Contents

Acknowledgements

We wish to thank the Nottingham University Writers' Group and Diabetes UK for helpful comments; Paul, Madeleine and Lydia Johnson for their encouragement, support and inspiration in countless ways and David Leicester and Jane Dover for particular ideas. Thanks, too, to Jean and Robert Maltby and Dr Chris Hall. Finally, very warm thanks to Karen Langley for her unfailing patience and hard work in preparing the manuscript.

Mal Leicester and Gill Johnson

Gill Johnson would like to thank Mal Leicester: it has been a privilege to work with her on this book.

Stories for Inclusive Schools

ary school teacher. Packed
provides a wealth of activi-

and inspiring approach to
es into classroom learning.
such sensitive areas as:

s

ect for diversity, enhance
s to key skills learning in
and concentrating. Many
lls, numeracy and science

ential tool for teachers or
or all children throughout

ottingham University. She
Classroom and Assembly

Gill Johnson has taught in primary schools in London and Nottingham, and has recently completed an MA in Children's Literature at the University of Nottingham.

CHILDREN

If children live with criticism
They learn to condemn

If children live with hostility
They learn to fight

If children live with ridicule
They learn to be shy

If children live with shame
They learn to feel guilty

If children live with tolerance
They learn to be patient

If children live with encouragement
They learn confidence

If children live with praise
They learn to appreciate

If children live with fairness
They learn justice

If children live with security
They learn to have faith

If children live with approval
They learn to like themselves

If children live with acceptance and friendship
They learn to find love in the world

Stories for Inclusive Schools

Developing young pupils' skills in assembly
and in the classroom

Mal Leicester and Gill Johnson

 RoutledgeFalmer
Taylor & Francis Group

LONDON AND NEW YORK

First published 2004
by RoutledgeFalmer
11 New Fetter Lane, London EC4P 4EE

Simultaneously published in the USA and Canada
by RoutledgeFalmer
29 West 35th Street, New York, NY 10001

*RoutledgeFalmer is an imprint of
the Taylor & Francis Group*

© 2004 Mal Leicester and Gill Johnson
© 2004 1(a) – 6(a) Mal Leicester
© 2004 1(b) – 6(b) Gill Johnson

Typeset in Times New Roman by GreenGate Publishing Services,
Tonbridge, Kent
Printed and bound in Great Britain by TJ International Ltd,
Padstow, Cornwall

British Library Cataloguing in Publication Data
A catalogue record for this book is available from the British
Library

Library of Congress Cataloging in Publication Data
A catalog record for this book has been requested

ISBN 0–415–31112–8

Introduction

Story and inclusive education

Stories for Inclusive Schools follows the recently published *Stories for Classroom and Assembly*. Both books share an engaging approach and a flexible format but they differ in focus and content. The learning focus of this second book interrelates:

- unlearning prejudice
- exploring difference
- dealing with bullying.

And though the different stories and learning activities of each book are underpinned by the same humane and liberal values (such as valuing empathy, compassion, tolerance *and* self-esteem) each collection stands independently. Similar but separate, the two books are fraternal rather than identical twins. The first covered the general cross-curricular themes (personal, social, moral, spiritual and emotional development) while the second is more specifically focused on developing the skills and values appropriate to an *inclusive* education.

There is much emphasis on 'educational inclusion' at the moment. But how can teachers ensure that children of all kinds feel welcome and 'at home' in their mainstream school? For 'different' children to be successfully 'integrated' we need teacher awareness about bullying and who is likely to be bullied; about how to recognise and relate to vulnerable children; about how to develop all the children's attitudes and values towards diversity/difference/inclusion. Mainstream children need to develop understanding and acceptance. The 'different' child himself or herself needs to acquire a positive self-image, self-respect and confidence.

This book is for use at Key Stage Two but can readily be adapted for Key Stage One. It is a more demanding collection than was *Stories for Classroom and Assembly*. In keeping with the complexities of inclusive education, the stories incorporate difficult issues, reflect painful emotions and are followed by more complex learning activities. The children in these stories face prejudice, bullying and the experience of 'being different'. However, it is because we use stories, and, moreover, stories *such* that young pupils can readily identify with the central characters, that teachers will be able to explore, in safety, these otherwise 'scary' aspects of their pupils' world.

The nature of story

Story-telling has always been a powerful and basic human activity. 'In all civilisations and cultures, both the activity of story-telling and significant, individual stories have been passed down the generations. This is because, long before the printed word was available, story was the means by which people attempted to make sense of their experience of the world, to communicate that understanding and to achieve a collective wisdom through passing on accumulating knowledge and values in a memorable and accessible way.' (Leicester 2003).

Stories help us to understand why we act as we do. Crucially, they enable us to explore even painful human interactions in an enjoyable way. They both *educate* and *entertain*. Thus, stories, used well, become a powerful classroom resource. Children can explore their own painful experiences through telling their own stories. Moreover, through recognising their own experience in the stories of others, they can make sense of their experience in a space which is both personal and objective.

Indeed, used by a good teacher stories can:

- stimulate the children's thinking and imagination

- encourage discussion

- encourage cooperative learning activities

- reveal a variety of points of view

- encourage self knowledge

- teach about the world in which they live

- introduce the complex realm of values

- develop positive attitudes.

Above all, the use of story is important in the development of empathy. 'Narratives not only help to humanise aliens, strangers and scapegoats – as Harriet Beecher Stowe's *Uncle Tom's Cabin* did, for example, regarding white prejudices against blacks – but also to make each one of us into an "agent of love" sensitive to the particular details of others' pain and humiliation' (Rorty).

For all these reasons we believe that story is important in the education of young children and is an excellent way to approach this particular task of education for inclusion. Stories should be engaging, subtle, indirect, rather than directly didactic. Stories can simultaneously influence the attitudes of 'mainstream' or ordinary children and the self-esteem of the 'different' child. ('Mainstream'/'different' are not absolute categories. A given child is sometimes one and sometimes the other. Thus a black child, for example, could be negative towards a bald child, or an overweight child negative towards a 'poor' child.) Stories can readily be used to generate associated educational activities which not only promote cognitive development but which also address emotional and values education. Indeed the importance of stories in the development of our shared values is often overlooked. No 'different' child will be embarrassed by the story (or associated activities) in the collection since the values education dimension is integral and subtle.

Prejudice, bullying and learning

As children and even as adults, we are all potential victims of bullying. (Indeed, the incidence of bullying at work is surprisingly high.) Though weaker and more vulnerable children are more likely to be victims, a child could be bullied precisely because he or she is seen as extra privileged or gifted or strong. It is the perception of someone as 'different' or 'other' that often triggers excluding behaviour. This is why dealing with bullying is part of inclusive education. An inclusive education which teaches children to be interested rather than threatened by 'difference', and to unlearn endemic social prejudice, will tend to reduce the incidence of bullying in school, and, ultimately, in the wider society.

However, having acknowledged that any child could be a victim of bullying, it is important that teachers recognise the kinds of children that may be at particular risk. Children who come new to the school must be monitored for bullying. Have they found a welcoming ethos and a friendly atmosphere? Have they been 'shown the ropes' by teachers and classmates and have they made some friends?

Children from minority groups may also be at risk. We know from research and countless social surveys that there are endemic prejudices in our society – widespread myths and stereotypes against various minority groups, including ethnic minorities, disabled people, older people, women etc. These prejudices often make members of these social groups, including children from minority ethnic groups and disabled children, more vulnerable to discrimination (individual and institutional) including, in school, to bullying.

However, there are also some forms of 'difference' which are less obvious or less acknowledged and which have received less 'academic' and less 'educational' attention. We have identified (below) six categories of such 'different' vulnerable children. Thus we ensure that our notion of 'inclusiveness' includes but goes beyond ethnicity and disability to cover other kinds of exclusion.

Though children often blame themselves for being bullied, it should never be regarded as the child's own fault. All schools should have guidelines for dealing with bullying. (See, for example, *Children's Books about Bullying*, edited by Rosemary Stone. This provides details of books for children, parents and schools.) Teachers must also have an understanding of the causes of bullying. Children who regularly bully other children are often disturbed and unhappy children. They may be bullied or abused at home or have low self-esteem. These children, though often difficult, may be the most in need of our loving understanding.

The outsider and inclusive education

Children need to learn how to deal with bullying and some of the activities in this collection help them to do this. They must also be encouraged not to bully. To this end, the stories and activities also seek to develop the children's self-confidence and self-esteem. In addition, children need to recognise and unlearn the social prejudices which we have discussed. Some of the stories include children from the relevant social groups and some of the activities seek to develop relevant understanding and tolerance.

An inclusive education is partly about making all children feel welcome and at home in school and partly about helping all children to unlearn social prejudices (such as racial prejudice) and to resist the impulse to target 'the other', 'the outsider', or 'the different'. Our stories and activities seek to foster humane and liberal values of justice and care – developing empathy for others and open-minded interest in the variety of people and ways of life.

In doing this we will need to be sensitive in the terms we use, keeping up with changes (e.g. 'a child has epilepsy' rather than 'an epileptic') and when in doubt, selecting terms to refer to people which that group itself prefers.

To these ends, the stories and activities focus on *six* 'outsider' categories as follows:

(1) Alternative lifestyles

As a way into considering alternative lifestyles, we have a story involving travellers and one involving the waterways. Children whose background involves a non-mainstream way of life may be seen as 'the other' – particularly when the lifestyle is subject to widespread social prejudice. There has been a long history of persecution of 'gypsies' and the travelling community continues to experience prejudice and discrimination. It is part of a multicultural and inclusive education to counter this.

(2) Difference in appearance

As a way into considering difference in appearance, we have a story involving a bald child and one involving a child who wears glasses. We all tend to judge others by their appearance and to be influenced by image and fashion and 'cool'. Not surprisingly, children are easily influenced by these things. What they themselves and others look like, particularly in the eyes of their peer group, is of considerable importance. Those children who do not conform to the acceptable 'norm' can be hurt by insensitivity and may even be bullied as readily distinguishable victims.

(3) Ethnic diversity: colour and culture

As a way into racism and ethnic prejudice, we have a story about a Muslim child and one which explores colour difference through sci-fi. Though there is now much recognition in schools that a good education will be multicultural and will endorse racial equality, nevertheless, prejudice about and discrimination against minority ethnic groups remains a reality. This racism is sometimes based on colour and sometimes on culture. It is important for the whole school to develop a curriculum permeated by cultural diversity and school structures which do not disadvantage cultural minorities. In thinking about being welcoming and inclusive and about countering bullying, we wanted to include two stories which will allow some direct discussion of such issues.

(4) Integrating disabled children

As a contribution to the successful inclusion of disabled children in mainstream school, we include a story about a blind boy and one about a child with autism. Post Warnock there has been increasing recognition that where possible, children with special needs should be integrated into mainstream schooling. There are various forms of integration (link schemes, project-based, special units, etc.) It need not be an 'all-or-nothing' affair. It has also been recognised, however, that for disabled children to be successfully included in mainstream provision, there are implications for the attitudes of all the teachers and pupils involved. We need to counter endemic prejudice against disabled children – whose wellbeing requires a genuine welcome. They should be welcomed for who they are. They need to find an inclusion free from being bullied or patronised – a welcoming integration on equal terms.

(5) Hidden disability

As a way into examples of 'hidden disability' we have included a story about a pupil who has diabetes and one about a child who has HIV.

Children who have less obvious 'disabilities' may nevertheless have a condition which may affect their learning or their wellbeing in school. For example, they may tire easily and require rest room facilities, or they may need special medication about which they should not need to feel embarrassed. They may be partially sighted or delicate, emotionally disturbed or hyperactive, have epilepsy or diabetes or be highly gifted. In an inclusive school, all these children will be catered for in matter-of-fact, practical ways in an ethos of acceptance.

In the case of the story *A Secret*, about a child who has HIV … it is very much a matter of professional judgement as to how much or how little information is used or discussed in relation to HIV/Aids. For younger children it may be more appropriate to focus on the issue of keeping secrets.

(6) Parental difference: recognising all families

As a way into examples of 'different' family structures and circumstances, we have included a story about a very 'poor' (low-income) family and one about a one parent family (a father).

Another way in which a child may appear as 'different' is through his or her family background. For example, his or her family might be richer or poorer, or differently structured, than those of most of her classmates. There are many different kinds of 'family' – one parent, two gay parents, an extended family, grandmother as carer, foster family, families with a step parent, etc. Indeed, the traditional two parent nuclear family is becoming much less of a norm. It is important that schools recognise all families as families – both in practical terms and in attitudes and values adopted and conveyed.

Transcending all these different categories of difference are the following key points:

- all children have the right to a happy and effective schooling;

- an inclusive school will cater for all pupils – in its structures, through its values and in the ethos developed;

- children who are perceived as different may be more vulnerable to bullying;

- children often keep painful experiences to themselves, they may blame themselves, but bullying is never their fault;

- an inclusive school will deal effectively to discourage, prevent and deal with prejudice and bullying;

- the use of story is a good 'way in'.

How to use this book

Twelve new stories are grouped into pairs. Each pair of stories focuses on an aspect of inclusive education. Thus the six aspects covered are as follows:

(1) Including alternative lifestyles:

    (a) Travellers
    (b) Waterways.

(2) Including a variety of minority ethnic group issues:

    (a) Muslim prejudice
    (b) Colour prejudice.

(3) Including 'difference' in appearance:

    (a) Bald/sparse hair
    (b) Wearing glasses.

(4) Including disabled children:

    (a) A blind child
    (b) A child with autism.

(5) Including children with hidden conditions:

    (a) Diabetes
    (b) HIV.

(6) Including different kinds of family:

    (a) One parent (father)
    (b) Low income family.

Flexibility

Each of these twelve stories is the focus for one teaching session. The twelve sessions should be used to suit your teaching schedule. For example, you could use one session per week for twelve weeks. Each session provides a story, some points for discussion, and follow up associated educational activities. Though approximate times are suggested for these activities, obviously you should set a pace which suits you and your class.

The intention is to save you time by providing good 'inclusive' material for classroom work and for the school assembly, but you can be flexible in how you use this material. For instance, you may prefer a different sequence – perhaps because some of the later stories link with work you are currently doing and therefore could be used first.

The sessions

- Having introduced the theme of the story you can tell *or* read it.

- The children could sit in a circle for the story and discussion time.

- Deal with 'difficult' vocabulary in your usual way. This is often to explain words as you come to them in the story.

- You may or may not want to ask the *closed* (comprehension-type) questions to check understanding. You may want to ask some of them as you read, or only after you have finished reading, or not at all.

- You can select or add to the more *open* 'points for discussion' – according to those aspects of the theme most relevant to your curriculum.

- You can select or add to the suggested activities. Some activities could be used in follow-up lessons.

● You may wish to use the classroom activity partly as preparation for the relevant assembly. Suggestions are given.

● Also for the assembly, suggested poems and songs are given. The suggestions are taken from commonly used texts. However, should you have different poetry and songbooks in your school, you will find that it is not difficult to find poems and songs which are relevant to the themes. One of the activities for each session encourages the children themselves to make this selection – an educative task!

● You can involve the children as active participants in the assembly to different degrees, commensurate with the custom in your school.

● You can link the themes with each other and with other on-going projects. For example, the stories/sessions in themes one and two will contribute to multicultural education; themes three and four to the integration of disabled children, including link projects; themes five and six to family learning projects.

The curriculum

You will find that as well as having a particular focus on inclusive education, each session also contributes to key skills in English (as you would expect, given the valuing of story). Thus each session involves such skills as speaking and listening, reflecting, reasoning and concentrating. Many of the activities also develop coordination skills and art and craft work and some highlight numeracy. In addition, the stories make an implicit contribution to multicultural education. They contain children of various ethnic origins and reflect respect for diversity. More broadly, they will be part of your values education – encouraging children to 'unlearn' prejudice and to develop more positive attitudes to themselves and to others. Stories, discussion and activities all have regard for the encouragement of critical thought *and* the stimulation of the imagination.

Most importantly, the resource will make an excellent contribution to dealing with bullying in your school – further developing a welcoming ethos.

Age levels

The material is intended for use at Key Stages One and Two. Since this includes a relatively wide age range (4–11 years) you will obviously use the material at the developmental level appropriate for your children. Thus a class of younger children will 'tell' rather than 'write' their own stories and learn to recognise key words. Older children, on the other hand, will be able to write their own associated stories and poems and may even take a turn in reading part of the theme story in classroom or assembly.

Precious time

The book is intended to be a useful and *time-saving* resource for classroom and assembly. I am sure that, like all learning/teaching resources it will be used in a whole variety of different ways. Some teachers may reach for the book as the basis for a morning's work on those (rare but inevitable!) occasions when they have simply not had time to prepare material of their own. Other teachers may take each story/activity as the starting point for an extended project on the highlighted theme (or it may be their turn to prepare an assembly). Some schools may wish to use the resource in a whole-school approach against prejudice and bullying. They may encourage parents to use the book to work with their child. The book could provide bedtime or rainy day stories with the bonus of discussion points and associated educational activities. In whatever way you choose to use it, we hope that you and the children will enjoy the theme-stories and the activities and that these will genuinely promote the development of those worthwhile values, skills and attitudes which should be part of a balanced education.

References

Stone R. (Ed.) (1998) *Children's Books about Bullying*. The Reading and Language Information Centre.

Leicester M. (2003) *Stories for Classroom and Assembly: Active Learning in Values Education at Key Stages One and Two*. Routledge/Falmer.

Jumping the Pipes

Teacher's Notes

Theme One (a):   Alternative Lifestyles (Travellers)

Inclusive Education: Unlearning prejudice against the travelling community is part of **Inclusive Education**

> If the children of travellers are to feel welcome at school we need to counter endemic prejudices against the travelling community, and, of course, to develop a school ethos against bullying.

Lesson Plan

This five-part lesson plan is only a guide. Teachers are likely to add to or amend the learning activities which are suggested and may sometimes wish to substitute their own. For any part of the session they may wish to allow more or less time than that suggested.

1 Introduce the theme   *5 minutes*

The story is about two boys: Dan, who is bullied because he is small and Joss, whose parents are travellers and who comes to Dan's school.
What bullying is and why it is wrong.
What do we know about the travelling community?

2 Vocabulary   *5 minutes*

The teacher ensures that the children understand the words given.

3 The story   *5–10 minutes*

The teacher shows the illustration and reads the story.

4 Talking about the story   *10–15 minutes*

The teacher uses some of the questions and discussion points given, stimulating the children to talk about the story/theme.

5 The learning activity   *20–25 minutes*

Learning activities are suggested. One could be selected and others used in subsequent, follow-up lessons.

Total time   *45–60 minutes*

1 INTRODUCE THE THEME

Key points

● At this point we want the children to understand the concept of bullying. What it is (to make someone unhappy or frightened on purpose) and what kinds of forms it can take. Give examples and ask the children for examples too. (Verbal bullying e.g. name-calling, emotional bullying e.g. leaving out, physical bullying e.g. hitting, kicking, throwing stones.) It is widespread (50% of children are bullied). If you are bullied, it is never your fault.

● At this point we want the children to know that travellers move around because this is their way of life. We all have the right to choose our own way of life provided that we don't hurt or bully other people by the way in which we live. Give examples of other alternative ways of life (e.g. living on the waterways or in a lighthouse or in a commune or 'residential' college).

---

2 VOCABULARY

Use your usual methods for introducing new words.

The difficult words/references in the story are:

designing   –   *making a pleasing pattern or plan*

jeering   –   *mocking*

taunts   –   *insults*

scarpered   –   *ran away*

pedlar   –   *someone who goes from house to house selling small things*

promise   –   *vow; solemn undertaking*

3 THE STORY:

Jumping the Pipes

Jumping the Pipes

One day, as Dan Todd was designing an old-fashioned gypsy caravan on his computer, he heard the muffled thud of a ball being kicked about in the street outside. Crossing to his bedroom window Dan gazed down at six boys who were trying to score goals in a makeshift goal post made from jumpers weighted down with stones. Dan watched the game and longed to join in, but one of the boys was Hawks, the school bully. Hawks often picked on Dan.

In the end though, Dan ran downstairs and out towards the game. Hawks shouted, "Look who's here. Tadpole Todd."

Six boys with jeering faces turned to stare at Dan who came to a halt, statue-still, uncertain what to do.

"Shove off shorty," Hawks yelled, picking up a stone and throwing it as hard as he could. Dan felt a sharp sting on his leg and seeing Hawks bend again he turned and ran, fearing the whack of another stone on his back. He slowed down only when he was out of range and could no longer hear the taunts and laughter which followed him.

Dan headed for the pipes which he had discovered in the fields behind the houses – six round, concrete pipes, each about two and a half metres long and just over one metre high, which lay side by side. You could run through each pipe or climb up to jump from one to the next. Whenever Dan felt lonely and sad, as he did now, he liked to go jumping the pipes.

Dan reached the wide, shallow stream that bordered the field of pipes. He watched the clean, bright water ripple round the rocks in its path. He found the place where he knew that several large stones rose above the water. Carefully he stepped from stone to stone, reaching the far side with satisfaction.

Now Dan could see the pipes and he saw that a young boy was standing on top of the first. The child, who was only about three years old, was sobbing as though his heart would break. Dan ran over as fast as he could.

"I'm stuck," the child wailed.

"Don't worry," said Dan, "just stand still a minute."

Dan climbed up beside the boy and helped him to sit down.

"Now sit still," he said.

Dan jumped back down and stood in front of him, reaching up to clasp his waist.

"OK, just slide down. Don't worry, I've got you."

Screwing closed his eyes the small child allowed his body to slide down the pipe. Fortunately, tough blue jeans protected his legs from being scratched and Dan held him firmly, helping him to land safely, feet on the ground.

"I want to go home," said the child immediately, his face still wet from his tears. He pointed to a distant field where Dan could see what looked like several big white vans.

Dan took the boy's hand and walked him home. Some of the white vans turned out to be modern caravans. It was a traveller's campsite. Dan knew that some people in his street didn't like the travellers, but Dan couldn't understand why. Mrs Meanie, who lived next door to Dan, said that they were dirty, but the caravans were gleaming and there was no litter about the site at all. Dan thought it must be great fun, travelling on from place to place and not going to school with a bully like Hawks.

Seeing the young child, a dark boy came running towards them. Like Dan he was about eight years old but as tall for his age as Dan was short.

"There you are Ryan. Thank God!"

"I found him stuck on the pipes," Dan explained. "He'd climbed up but couldn't get down."

"But I did slided right down," said Ryan proudly, sloping his small hand like a slide.

"Thanks," the tall boy said to Dan. "I only just realised he'd scarpered. We was waiting by the van-school for our go."

"The van-school?" asked Dan.

The boy pointed to a large van with 'Avon Education Authority' on the side.

"It's my go next," he said.

"A school in a van," said Dan. "Wow. My school's closed today."

"They want me to go to your school," said the boy. "Cos we're stopping here for a while. I dunno though."

He had an unusual way of talking which Dan liked.

"I'd love to see your van-school," Dan said.

The boy nodded in the direction of the van.

"Come on then, I'll ask Miss."

The teacher, Miss Williams, was really nice. She let Dan in with the tall boy, who was called Joss. Ryan, who was Joss's kid brother, came in too. Dan gazed round in amazement. Inside the van it was just like a real classroom. There were three desks, cupboards full of books, and bright posters on the sides.

"Each pair of children has just one hour," Miss Williams explained to Dan.

"We like it," Joss told him.

"Yes Joss, but you could have more time at the proper school," Miss Williams said.

Dan enjoyed that hour enormously. First Miss Williams read a poem from a book. The poem was called *The Pedlar's Caravan*, by W B Rands and it reminded Dan of the picture he had been working on.

"That was great," he said.

"Now you read it Dan," said Miss Williams. Dan read *The Pedlar's Caravan*.

"I wish I lived in a caravan,
With a horse to drive like a pedlar-man!
Where he comes from nobody knows,
Nor where he goes to, but on he goes.

His caravan has windows two,
With a chimney of tin that the smoke comes through,
He has a wife, and a baby brown,
And they go riding from town to town."

After that, Miss Williams gave Joss, Dan and Ryan a sheet of paper each and some coloured pencils. She asked them to draw the poem's old-fashioned caravan with its horse. As they sketched and coloured Dan answered questions about his school.

"I get picked on by the horrid Hawks because I'm small," he said at the end.

Joss called Hawks a swear name and Miss Williams frowned at him.

"Sorry Miss. But what a nutter – picking on someone just because he's small," Joss said, scornfully.

"You'd be alright Joss. Hawks wouldn't pick on you. You're too big," said Dan. "Do come, I'll show you how everything works."

"Would you help me with the lessons, Dan, just at first?"

"Sure," said Dan, "you bet."

"Promise," said Joss, solemnly.

"I promise," said Dan.

They had finished their pictures by now. Dan had used some of the ideas from his computer design. His caravan was decorated with a colourful pattern. The smoke from his chimney looked like real smoke and his horse was glossy black and beautiful.

"That's brilliant," said Joss.

"You can have it if you want," Dan said, shyly.

"Thanks," said Joss. He took the picture looking pleased.

Later, outside the van-school, Dan knew he must say goodbye. He didn't want to leave his new friend but his mum would be worried if he wasn't home by four o'clock.

"Bye Joss," he said. "Bye Ryan."

"I'll see you at the other school then," said Joss. "On Monday. I'll give it a try."

Dan was really pleased to hear that.

"And listen Dan," said Joss, grinning. "No one will bully you again mate. It's my turn to promise and I promise you that."

4 TALKING ABOUT THE STORY

Did the children understand?

- What is an old-fashioned gypsy caravan?

- Why did Dan feel lonely and sad at the beginning?

- Why could Joss now go to 'proper' school?

- What helped Dan to draw such a good picture?

- What did Dan promise Joss and what did Joss promise Dan?

Points for discussion

- **The nature of bullying**
  In what ways did Hawks bully Dan? (Physical – stone throwing, and verbal – name-calling.) Discuss what is wrong with the different forms of bullying – verbal, emotional, physical – and how they cause hurt. Try to bring out that anyone can be bullied, but no one deserves to be, it is not their fault.

- **Difference**
  Hawks picked on Dan because he was short. Bullying is cowardly because the bully usually picks on someone *vulnerable* – weaker or smaller or younger or disabled. Bullies often pick on people they think are *different* – a different colour or background etc. In fact we are *all* different and that makes us more interesting.

- **What can we do about bullying?**
  Avoid bullies. Ignore name-calling. Try to be self-confident. If the bullying is persistent – *tell an adult you trust*: parent, teacher, headteacher, classroom assistant.

5 THE LEARNING ACTIVITY

Links

i)   The activities link with the story through the children's increasing understanding of travellers and also of bullying.

ii) The assembly connects with the story through valuing tolerance and kindness.

iii) If you wish to link the activity to the assembly, one or more of the children could read their chosen poem. Or, some of the best of the 'advice' letters could be read. The drawings of the children who chose to do an old-fashioned gypsy caravan could be displayed in the assembly hall.

ACTIVITY SUGGESTIONS

1 CHOOSING AN ACTIVITY LINKED TO THE STORY

(A) Let the children:

● Draw (or paint) an old-fashioned caravan as Dan did.

or

● Write a story about Joss at Dan's school.

Resources needed

Colouring pencils or paint

(B) Poetry:

● Write a poem called 'The Pedlar's Caravan'.

or

● In pairs or in small groups, find a poem or song which connects with the story. It could be about travellers or travelling, or about bullying or (by contrast) about kind, welcoming behaviour. It could be about finding a new friend or rescuing someone, as Dan did. After some reading time, ask some of the children to read their poem (or song) and to explain its link with the story *Jumping the Pipes*.

Resources needed

Poetry and/or song books

2 LEARNING ABOUT TRAVELLERS

First, tell the children about travellers.

● Long ago all people were travellers. In Britain it was about 5,000 years ago that some people settled into permanent dwellings.

● Some travellers, who speak the Romany language, travelled across Europe, bringing to Britain new music, dances, arts and crafts. These people used to be called gypsies.

● There are different kinds of travellers who move around doing different kinds of work – agricultural labour, scrap or car dealing, fairgrounds.

● Some travellers stay for a while on accommodation sites (like Joss's family). Some sites have good facilities (like water and local schools) and some have poor facilities.

- Travellers were persecuted in the sixteenth and seventeenth centuries and some sedentary (that is, 'settled') people still dislike travellers and, because of this prejudice, sometimes make them move on. That is why getting education or health care can be difficult for some travellers.

Second, in small groups or pairs, the children could talk about the advantages and disadvantages of a travelling life and of a settled life. What would they like and dislike about each?

Third, as a whole class again, make a list on the blackboard of the advantages and disadvantages of a travelling lifestyle, taking the suggestions from the children.

3 FOCUS ON BULLYING (GETTING ADVICE)

Teacher: 'Pretend Dan and Hawks are in your class. Write a letter to a children's helpline. Explain how Hawks bullies Dan and ask for advice about what you should do to help Dan.'

When the children have written their letters, ask them to pretend to be the helpline advisor.

They should write the reply to their first letter, and give advice about what to do.

4 FINAL DISCUSSION

Later you could read out the letters which give good and useful advice, and discuss these. You could also give the children the address and telephone number of some advice lines. For example:

Kidscape
152 Buckingham Palace Road
London
SW1W 9TR
Tel: 020 7730 3300
Mon-Fri 10.00 am to 4.00 pm

Helpline for parents of bullied or bullying children.
Send an SAE for three free booklets about bullying.

Free Helplines (won't show up on the telephone bill)
Child Line   0800 1111
Samaritans   0345 909090

Assembly

Theme: Tolerance and Kindness

Introduction

The assembly leader introduces the themes of tolerance and kindness. We should be interested in children who are different from ourselves, not prejudiced against them. We feel better about ourselves when we treat others with kindness. We don't really like ourselves when we bully.

Story

Assembly leader

'Our story today is about Dan, who though he was bullied himself, was strong enough not to be a bully. Instead we see that he is a kind boy who makes friends with an interesting traveller child called Joss.'

The assembly leader reads the story – *Jumping the Pipes*.

You can choose a poem or a song or both. Alternatively, you can have a child (or children) read the poems they chose or wrote in class and have one of the songs that were chosen. Select poems and songs which are relevant to the theme or which echo the story in some way.

Poem or song

Examples

Poems:

Use the full *The Pedlar's Caravan* poem.

I wish I lived in a caravan,
With a horse to drive like a pedlar-man!
Where he comes from nobody knows,
Nor where he goes to, but on he goes.

His caravan has windows two,
With a chimney of tin that the smoke comes through,
He has a wife, and a baby brown,
And they go riding from town to town.

Chairs to mend and delf to sell –
He clashes the basins like a bell.
Tea-trays, baskets, ranged in order,
Plates, with the alphabet round the border.

The roads are brown, and the sea is green,
But his house is just like a bathing-machine.
The world is round, but he can ride,
Rumble, and splash to the other side.

With the pedlar-man I should like to roam,
And write a book when I come home.
All the people would read my book,
Just like the Travels of Captain Cook.

The Bully (feelings about being bullied)
Page 27 in *Poems About You and Me: A collection of poems about values*, compiled by Brian Moses, published by Wayland Publishers, 1998.

The Dolphin (fantasy travel)
Page 70 in *A Very First Poetry Book*, by John Foster, published by Oxford University Press, 1984.

Grandma Mabel (a kind grandma)
Page 44 in *Smile Please!* by Tony Bradman, published by Puffin, 1989.

Songs:

Every Colour Under the Sun (celebrating difference)
No. 16 in *Every Colour Under the Sun*, published by Ward Lock Educational Co. Ltd, 1983.

Moving on Song (meanly moving travellers on)
No. 39 in *Alleluya!* (2nd Edition), published by A&C Black, 1980.

Quiet reflection or prayer

For a universal, humanistic or multi-faith assembly:

Quiet reflection

The assembly leader says:
'Let us think about how it feels to be bullied and decide not to be a bully. If we are being bullied, let us think about who we could go to for help. (Pause) Let us remember someone who is kind and feel grateful for that person. (Pause) Finally, picture someone to whom you will be kind and friendly today.' (Pause)

Or for Christian schools:

Prayer

Dear Father,
Please give Your strength to anyone who is being bullied and help them to deal with it. And to anyone who is a bully, give them the strength to stop bullying. Thank you for kind people. Help us to be kind, strong and gentle today.

Amen.

Liveaboard About a Bit!

Teacher's Notes

Theme One (b): **Alternative Lifestyles (Waterways)**

Inclusive Education: Respecting differences in people's lifestyles is part of **Inclusive Education**

Children need to learn that alternative lifestyles are to be respected. An understanding and knowledge of alternative lifestyles can help children avoid building stereotypes.

Lesson Plan

This five-part lesson plan is only a guide. Teachers are likely to add to or amend the learning activities which are suggested and may sometimes wish to substitute their own. For any part of the session they may wish to allow more or less time than that suggested.

1 Introduce the theme *5 minutes*

A boy who lives on the waterways befriends another boy at school, who also feels a little bit on the outside of city life. The boys spend a weekend enjoying the waterways together.

2 Vocabulary *5 minutes*

The teacher ensures that the children understand the words given – usually within the context of the story as it is being read.

3 The story *5–10 minutes*

The teacher shows the illustration and reads the story.

4 Talking about the story *10–15 minutes*

The teacher uses some of the questions and discussion points given, stimulating the children to talk about the story/theme.

5 The learning activity *20–25 minutes*

Learning activities are suggested. One could be selected and others used in subsequent, follow-up lessons.

Total time *45–60 minutes*

1   INTRODUCE THE THEME

Key points

● Children need to build up an understanding of alternative lifestyles so that they can develop respect for the different ways in which people choose to live. A genuine understanding of alternative lifestyles means that children can challenge stereotypes that may be presented to them.

2   VOCABULARY

Use your usual methods for introducing new words.

The difficult words/references in the story are:

falafel	–	*a deep-fried ball of ground chick-peas, with onions, peppers, garlic and spices; popular in North Africa*
'liveaboards'	–	*people who live afloat on canals or rivers; some cruise continuously, some are permanently moored and others do a mixture*
moonwalking	–	*a dance step which creates the illusion of sliding effortlessly along the floor*
Jamaica	–	*an island in the Caribbean*
silhouette	–	*the outline of a solid figure as made by its shadow*
tow-path	–	*a path alongside canals and some rivers for horses to pull barges or narrow boats*
persuasion	–	*making someone agree to something*
bantering	–	*having a good-humoured joking or teasing conversation*
ochre	–	*a yellow-orange colour*

3 THE STORY:

Liveaboard About a Bit

The Story

Liveaboard About a Bit!

I love Camden Lock; it's one of my best places to moor. The market's brilliant: so many people, so much colour and so many delicious smells! I especially like it at night – dad and I wander round chatting to everyone and sometimes if dad isn't in the mood to cook we'll buy jacket potatoes or spicy falafels that come in a big, flat bread.

I think I'm really lucky. I live on a narrow boat with my dad, Jez, and we travel from place to place. Not as much as when I was small because dad doesn't want me to have to change schools too often, but I've still travelled round more than most children I talk to. I never get bored: there's always so much to see and always something that needs doing with the boat. Not many children can say that their house floats!

Dad gets casual work as we travel about. What he *really* likes to do is paint pictures – usually of the waterways and other live-aboards and sometimes he gets to sell them. He always sells lots of paintings in the market here. Most of the time though, dad just takes whatever work is going. Dad seems to have so many friends. There's always someone that needs something doing! He helps lots of people out without charging them, especially other liveaboards who need help with repairs. I always feel really proud of him then.

If there's any money spare, dad usually buys me some new sheet music (I'm teaching myself the guitar) and he'll buy himself some new art stuff, special paper, paints and brushes.

I started back at school a few weeks ago. It always feels strange when I first walk in! Lots of faces I recognise but every-one has changed and I always feel like the outsider. That's the time when I wish I wasn't a liveaboard. I suddenly have this heavy feeling that I want to belong somewhere properly. It usually passes and I've talked to dad about it, because I feel guilty that I feel like that. Dad's totally cool about it and we talk about friends and loyalty and needing to belong and also the need to feel free – and I've never had a problem with that!

There are always a few children who give me funny looks and then what's worse, they look at their friends and give *them* funny looks about me. The head teacher is really nice and always welcomes me back as if I was a long lost friend, which I suppose I am. A few of the children welcome me back too at playtime and that's always really great. They like to hear all the news from the waterways: where I've been, what other schools I've been to, what the boat's like. Dad says I'm a bit of a natural storyteller, so if I've got everyone's attention I usually make the most of it. On the second day back, I was describing the boat and this one boy couldn't help smiling when I was talking about it.

"Man, that sounds so cool! Your boat sounds seriously wicked!"

"I reckon it is, where d'you live then?" I asked, chuffed that he liked the sound of my boat.

"Jeez, I'm in those flats man, it's like a chicken coop up there! I'm gonna be breaking out soon."

He erupted in laughter thinking of himself escaping from his cramped world. He had the sort of laugh that you couldn't help joining in with. It bubbled up from right inside him and made everyone else laugh too.

"What's your name then? I don't remember you from the last time I was here."

"Marcus's ma name and groovin's my game!" Marcus started laughing again. He started moonwalking and spinning: he looked like one of these dancers that you see on *Top of the Pops*.

"And what's your name, man?" asked Marcus as he stopped to catch his breath.

"Jake." I answered, then jokingly tried to moonwalk as Marcus had just done.

"Hey, that's not bad you know, you could learn my moves!"

It was my turn to laugh: the thought of me, moonwalking round school. I thought I stood out as it was, with my different clothes and longer hair. Lots of the children seemed to talk about labels and what trainers they were buying next. That didn't mean much to me: I didn't really care to be honest, but I'd never say that in the playground.

Over the next two weeks I got to know Marcus quite well. I think he felt a bit like a fish out of water too because he'd just come over from Jamaica to live with his mum. He loved his mum but he hated the flat and he missed his grandma and lazy evenings on the beach hanging out with his friends, fishing and messing about in the sea. Camden Lock didn't have quite the same appeal I suppose, especially on a day when it was rainy and miserable.

I'd had a growing thought that I wanted to ask dad if Marcus could join us on the boat for a weekend. I was surprised at myself thinking like that because I never expected to see school friends outside of school really. A bit of an outsider, as I said. Anyway, I talked to dad about it and he liked the idea.

"Sounds like a great idea Jake, as long as he doesn't mind the fold-down bed!"

I went into school on the Thursday feeling really excited for the first time in ages. I could hardly wait to see Marcus. He strutted in, with his usual carefree smile and beamed when he saw me.

"Hi Jake, how you doin'?"

"OK thanks. You alright?"

"Yeah, bit bored, that's all."

I felt nervous about asking Marcus for some reason, but I went for it anyway:

"D'you want to come on my boat this weekend? I asked my dad and he says it'd be OK."

"That is the *best* offer I've had since I been in this cold cramped up place."

"Will your mum let you come d'you think then?" I asked, still a bit nervous.

"Yeah, I reckon she be glad to have time out from me. But I'll check!"

"You'd have to sleep on a fold-down bed."

"There's cooped up in a flat and there's cooped up in a boat. Two *very* different things man!" I liked the way Marcus talked – he spoke with a lot of feeling in his voice which lots of the boys didn't have.

I could hardly wait for Friday to see what Marcus's mum said. As it happened, she walked him to school that morning, so I got to meet her. I was looking out for Marcus, like a cat on hot bricks.

"Hey, Jake you OK?"

"I'm fine, can you come?"

Marcus looked up at his mum with another of his beaming smiles.

"Yeah, it's cool."

"I'm Marcus's mum, Chantelle. It's really kind of you to invite Marcus on to your boat. Are you sure it's OK with your dad? I need to meet him anyway."

We made arrangements for Chantelle to meet my dad after school and then Marcus and I felt like we scootered through the day at full speed enjoying everything, because of what we had to look forward to.

That evening I felt like I would burst with excitement. Chantelle had met dad in the market after school and Marcus was going to get his bag together and join us at 6.30, in time to have tea before taking to the waters!

Marcus turned up at 6.15. He introduced me to a new food stand in the market which sold Caribbean food. Dad and I needed a break from falafels, so we were glad to try something different!

At 7.30 we were ready to go aboard and it felt very special showing Marcus round the boat. I could tell he really liked it and he seemed to be impressed at how everything fitted in so well.

"This boat is *totally* cool Jake, I *really* like it."

"We'll sit on deck for a bit, let's take our drinks with us."

Dad had made us a hot chocolate which tasted so good sitting on the deck, watching the light fade. There always seemed something magical to me about dusk. The silhouettes of the trees, branches outlined against the dark sky and people, walking ghost-like along the tow-path. It made me feel good inside though I could never find the words to explain to dad.

"That clear sky is just like Jamaica at night y'know; 'cept it'd be a bit warmer than this!"

Marcus chuckled as he dipped his head down deeper into his thick fleece.

We finished our hot chocolate and dad said we had better get some sleep, we would be setting off early in the morning and we had several locks to go through.

Marcus needed no persuasion to go to bed. He almost threw himself into his fold-down bed and wriggled into the quilt exaggerating how comfortable it was. He had so much energy and a sense of fun; he was good to have around.

I've heard dad talk about 'red letter days'; days that are special; days that stand out. I had two in a row with Marcus: a truly brilliant weekend. We woke up early on the Saturday and dad already had breakfast on the go.

"Thought some scrambled egg might keep us liveaboards going for a while."

"Sounds good to me, Mr Elliott!"

"You can call me Captain Jez, if you like!" joked dad.

Marcus squawked with laughter and said that he would look out for a hat for dad next time he went back to Jamaica.

After we'd cleared up the breakfast things, dad taught Marcus how to steer the narrow boat and talked him through what we would do when we came to a lock. Marcus proved to be a bit of a natural with steering and negotiating the locks. He followed dad's instructions really well.

We tied up after our third lock and had lunch, right in the middle of the city!

"I was hopin' to see London but I didn't expect to see it from a boat y'know," commented Marcus.

In the afternoon we got the bikes out and cycled along the tow-path; Marcus borrowed dad's bike. We had such a great time overtaking each other, cycling as fast as we could and then as slowly as we could. Dad was bantering with us from the boat, when we were near enough to hear him.

"Today, I do *not* feel like a cooped up chicken, I feel like a bird – them great big gliding ones. How 'bout you Jake?"

The boys at school would not have asked a question like that and I smiled at Marcus as I thought of an answer.

"Today, I'm the eagle soaring next to you – the sky is ours!!" I shouted the last bit with a "dramatic" voice, pedalling as fast as I could.

"You is a buddin' poet Jakey boy!"

After we had moored up for the night and had tea, Marcus and I messed about on my guitar with Marcus making up raps about life on the narrow boat. I couldn't stop laughing in between thinking of words.

Dad popped his head round to check out the squawks and the laughter.

"Are you composing in there or fighting off a bunch of crows?!" asked dad with a huge grin.

When we had calmed down enough we played dad our *Liveaboard About a Bit!* rap. Dad really liked it and dared us to play it for our teacher on Monday.

"Hmm, dat needs tinkin' 'bout," said Marcus. There was the natural bit of him which made everyone laugh but the idea of *performing* was another matter altogether.

On the Sunday, having made it as far as the Docklands, dad suggested that we turned around to give ourselves plenty of time to get back to Camden and we could stop off and have a go at some painting in between going through the locks.

Marcus was very keen on the painting idea, which was a relief. Some boys like football and nothing else. Marcus's auntie was a local artist in Jamaica so painting wasn't a strange idea to him.

Dad chose the spot carefully and we helped him set out the paints and mixing palettes. It was a beautiful morning with bright sunshine and the leaves looked like a collection of jewels in many colours: red, yellow, bronze and gold against the gloomier colour of the city buildings in the background.

We quickly became engrossed in what we were doing. Marcus painted how he laughed – with lots of energy. He plastered on the paint, creating some chunky textures on the paper. Dad teased him.

"Good job I didn't offer you water colours Marcus, I think they'd be wasted on you. You're definitely an oils man, I can see that!"

Dad held the tube of ochre paint over the pallette. "Another giant blob sir?!" he asked, pretending to be a waiter.

Marcus chuckled as he accepted another generous squirt of paint.

The afternoon disappeared into our colours and our pictures. Time melted away.

More cycling. Getting through the locks. Steering the boat. Pointing out the city sights. Watching the world go by. Another go at our rap.

By 6.30 we were back in Camden enjoying fish and chips. Chantelle was to collect Marcus at 7.30. Marcus and I sat on the boat, distanced from the bustle of the market.

"Thanks for coming Marcus!" I managed to say through a mouthful of fish, "I'm glad you like the boat."

"Jake, this weekend was so hot it was like being back in Jamaica!"

We both dissolved into fits of laughter yet again and whether it was on the strength of a new-found friendship or what, I don't know, but we decided to sing the rap for the class the following week! It went something like this:

Liveaboard about a bit!
Liveaboard about a bit!
Live a little
Float a little
Free as a bird
Free as a bird!

I'm callin' to you friend
As you walk along the path
C'mon and join our party
We've hardly even started

Liveaboard about a bit!
Liveaboard about a bit!
Live a little
Float a little
Free as a bird
Free as a bird!

TALKING ABOUT THE STORY

Did the children understand?

- What is a narrow boat?

- Why did Jake's dad decide not to travel quite so much?

- What appealed to Marcus about life on the waterways?

- What did Jake particularly appreciate about Marcus's personality?

Points for discussion

- What did Jake and his dad enjoy about life on the waterways?

- Why did Jake and Marcus feel that they had something in common?

- What can we do to welcome/include children who may have an alternative lifestyle, or who may simply feel different in some way?

- Have *you* ever felt distanced/different from other children for any reason? What did you do?

---

5 THE LEARNING ACTIVITY

Links

i)   The activities link with the story through the focus on appreciating different lifestyles.

ii) The assembly connects with the story through valuing differences in lifestyle.

iii) If you wish to link the activity to the assembly, one or more of the children could read their chosen poem or rap. Pictures of the narrow boats could be displayed in the assembly hall.

ACTIVITY SUGGESTIONS

1 CHOOSING AN ACTIVITY LINKED TO THE STORY

(A) Let the children:

- Look at the two photographs of the narrow boats.

- Copy the outline from one of the narrow boats and then add your own details to the boat design.

or

- Imagine you spend a weekend with a friend who is a liveaboard. Write a diary of your weekend.

Resources needed

Photocopy of narrow boats

(B) Poetry:

- Write a rap about something that makes you feel happy or good inside. Perhaps you could perform it to your classmates.

or

- Find a poem either individually or in a group which connects to or with the story. It could be about feeling happy, enjoying the water (rivers, canals or the sea), or friendship.

Resources needed

Poetry and/or song books

2 HOW DOES A LOCK WORK?

Older children or the more able could find out more about locks and how they work and share what they find out with the class.

Resources needed

A diagram of a lock
Books about canals/waterways

3 NARROW BOAT PAINTING

Children could explore the web for pictures of traditional artwork (roses and castles). Try to imitate the style of painting using thick paint in bright colours on dark paper.

Thick brushes are best to create the effect with bold brush strokes.

Resources needed

Thick brushes, thick paint and dark paper

Suggested websites:
www.canaljunction.com/folkrose.htm
www.josonja.com/guide/styles/traditional/canalboat.asp
www.canalia.co.uk/background

This narrow boat is waiting to be fitted out and painted.

A typical narrow boat moored on the canal.

Assembly

Theme: Alternative Lifestyles

Introduction

The assembly leader introduces the theme. Some people live in ways that are different from our own. We need to learn to value these differences.

Story

Assembly leader:

'Our story today is about a boy called Jake who lives on a narrow boat with his father. He is called a "liveaboard"'.

The assembly leader reads the story – *Liveaboard About a Bit!*

Poem or song

You can choose a poem or song or both. Alternatively, you can have a child (or children) read the poems they chose or wrote in class and have one of the songs that were chosen. Select poems and songs which are relevant to the theme or which echo the story in some way.

Examples

Poems:

Friendship (the quality of a good friend)
Page 11 in *Poems about You and Me: A collection of poems about values*, compiled by Brian Moses, published by Wayland Publishers, 1998.

Lonely Boy (feeling lonely)
Page 117 in *A First Poetry Book*, compiled by John Foster, published by Oxford University Press, 1979.

Legging the Tunnel (a grandfather's recollection of manoeuvring through a canal tunnel on a narrow boat)
Page 20 in *A Second Poetry Book*, compiled by John Foster, published by Oxford University Press, 1980.

Songs:

Happiness is (different ways of being happy)
No. 5 in *Alleluya!* (2nd Edition), published by A&C Black, 1980.

Points of View (difference of perspective)
No. 45 in *Every Colour Under the Sun*, published by Ward Lock Educational Co. Ltd, 1983.

Quiet reflection or prayer

For a universal, humanistic or multi-faith assembly:

Quiet reflection

The assembly leader says:
'Close your eyes for a moment, and think about the advantages of life on the waterways. (Pause) Think about your own way of living, and what you like about it. (Pause) Now think of someone who you can show kindness to today, who may be feeling on the outside of your school life, for whatever reason.' (Pause)

Or for Christian schools:

Prayer

Creator God,
We are so glad that You have made us as individuals who live our lives in different ways. Help us to understand and respect the different ways in which people live. Help us to learn that our differences are to be celebrated.

Amen.

Tales from the Beach

Teacher's Notes

Theme Two (a):	Difference in Appearances (and empathy)
Inclusive Education:	Developing tolerance to, and empathy about, differences in appearance is part of **Inclusive Education**

> Some children are sensitive about their appearance in some way – they may be shorter or taller than average, or thinner or fatter. They may wear glasses, or a tooth or body brace. They may have no hair or bright red hair or have a facial disfigurement. Because of this perceivable 'difference', they may be vulnerable to bullying. All the children need to learn to be sensitive to others' feelings about their appearance and accept people for their personality and character.

Lesson Plan

This five-part lesson plan is only a guide. Teachers are likely to add to or amend the learning activities which are suggested and may sometimes wish to substitute their own. For any part of the session they may wish to allow more or less time than that suggested.

1 Introduce the theme *5 minutes*

What is wrong with judging people by appearances? How do we show insensitivity to people's feelings about their appearance? (Give examples: e.g. staring, cruel remarks or 'jokes'.)

2 Vocabulary *5 minutes*

The teacher ensures that the children understand the words given.

3 The story *5–10 minutes*

The teacher shows the illustration and reads the story.

4 Talking about the story *10–15 minutes*

The teacher uses some of the questions and discussion points given, stimulating the children to talk about the story/theme.

5 The learning activity *20–35 minutes*

Learning activities are suggested. One could be selected and others used in subsequent, follow-up lessons.

Total time *45–60 minutes*

1 INTRODUCE THE THEME

Key points

- Children can readily understand about feeling self-conscious and could discuss this sympathetically.

- Introduce the distinction between appearance (as superficial characteristics) and character/personality (as being more central to who we are).

- Again children should understand that it is wrong to pick on people simply because of how they look.

- Introduce the idea of 'beauty' being relative to a culture and context.

2 VOCABULARY

Use your usual methods for introducing new words.

The difficult words/references in the story are:

conscious	–	*aware; awake; knowing what is happening*
sparsely	–	*thinly*
conceal	–	*hide*
post-traumatic shock	–	*feeling tense after a bad event*
malicious	–	*spiteful; wanting to harm others*
compliments	–	*praise; something you say to show admiration*
effectively	–	*successfully*
weaving	–	*threading in and out*
abandoned	–	*deserted; having gone away and left a person or place*
transformed	–	*changed*

3 THE STORY:

Tales from the Beach

Tales from the Beach

"Why must people stare?" she wondered, conscious that her hair, growing back so sparsely, failed to conceal the thin white scar which ran across one side of her scalp.

"I said, what do you think, Lucy?" Mr Cox repeated, and his eyes flicked again to her scar. "It's rude to stare sir," she felt like saying, but "I don't know sir," she muttered, instead.

Mr Cox gave an impatient sigh. "Detention, Monday," he snapped.

Lucy, still suffering post-traumatic shock and inclined to be tearful, blinked hard to keep from crying.

At break, as she was grumbling about Mr Cox to Helen, who was her best friend, Barb Willet came over.

"Like *your* hair Helen. What d'you think Lucy?" she said, staring at Lucy's shaved head. The two friends knew Barb of old. She was the most malicious girl in the school. She never paid compliments. Her remark to Helen was meant to be a hurtful dig at Lucy. Helen turned away from her.

"When do you go on holiday, Luce?" she said.

"Only a week to go now." Lucy spoke as cheerfully as she could to hide the hurt she felt inside. She, too, turned her back on Barb. "We want some sunshine, Helen. We've decided on The Gambia."

"Wow, Africa!" said Helen.

The two friends heard Barb, effectively snubbed, walk away. They smiled at each other.

"Thank God for Helen," Lucy thought. Dear Helen, who had told her how brave she had been about the operation and who knew, more than anyone, even her mum, how hard it was to have lost her long blonde hair.

Lucy had never been in a plane before. She stared down as it rose into the air. She saw London spread out below. She noticed the River Thames, its curves familiar from *Eastenders*, and saw a stream of cars, moving like toys in a row. Soon the plane entered a billowing sea of white clouds which glinted with sunlight. Lucy watched a film on a tiny TV screen set into the back of the seat in front of her and ate lunch off a plastic tray with little compartments for the orange juice and the pudding. By the time these trays were collected up, the plane had begun to descend. Her mum closed her eyes and gripped the arms of her seat and knowing she felt scared, Lucy patted her arm until the plane landed so smoothly that everyone gave the pilot a clap.

From the airport, a small bus took them to their holiday place and once there, the days sped by. Lucy and her mum enjoyed the sunshine and how friendly everyone was – the pale holiday-makers and the dark Gambian people. One day they were taken to see a pool of vegetarian crocodiles! Being a vegetarian herself, with a love of wild creatures, Lucy was very interested. She was actually allowed to pat one.

"Helen will never believe this," she thought.

But it was on the very last day that something even more amazing occurred. They had crossed the road to the long white beach near their holiday place and were watching the Gambian women weaving braids into each other's hair. One large lady with a red wrap round her own hair smiled at Lucy, who smiled back, shyly.

"I wish I could have braids with beads," she said, her voice full of longing.

The woman gestured for her to come nearer. Gently she tugged at Lucy's sparse hair. She spoke to one of the other women, who sent a young boy speeding off on an errand.

"He's gone to see if we can buy some yellow hair like yours," she said. She named the price for the hair and the braiding and Lucy's mum agreed immediately. It was a good price. The next twenty minutes passed very slowly for Lucy, who waited in almost painful hope. The boy returned and her heart leaped as she saw that he carried a plastic bag. Inside was the hair.

Lucy sat on a cane stool and the woman began, braiding the blond hair into Lucy's own. As she worked, the woman, who was called Ama, chatted non-stop, asking Lucy's mum about England, and telling them stories about the beach.

They enjoyed these tales. Lucy never forgot one of them, about a little brother and sister who were abandoned, on the beach, by their mother, because they had been born with green hair. They were adopted by a mermaid and went with her to live under the sea – where green hair was a sign of great beauty.

"Always remember, Lucy," Ama said, all the while still braiding her hair, "a thing may be proper in one place and yet another place may have a different proper."

Slowly, for it took several hours, Lucy's sparse, short hair was extended down to her shoulders. The blond braids covered her scar completely. Lucy moved her head and heard the lilac and turquoise beads click together. She loved the sound, and moved again, smiling. "Cool," she said.

"Thanks so much, Ama," said mum.

"Yes, thanks a million," said Lucy. She had been dreading going back to school but now, with her braids, felt quite differently about it and she was already looking forward to showing Helen.

Back at the holiday place, everyone admired her new hair, and Lucy, transformed, smiled until her face hurt.

4 TALKING ABOUT THE STORY

Did the children understand?

- How was Barb's 'compliment' to Helen really picking on Lucy?

- What did Ama mean when she said: 'a thing may be proper in one place and yet another place may have a different proper'?

Points for discussion

- **Why do people bully?**
  Barb was always malicious. Discuss why some people often bully others. (That they may be bullied themselves; that they feel bad about themselves; they are full of sadness or anger and take this out on others.)

- **A different 'proper'**
  Flying to other countries allows people to see that there are many different customs, cultures, forms of dress, food, etc. across the world. Differences of all kinds exist and can be interesting. What experiences or examples can the children suggest themselves of interesting differences in appearance or ways of doing things, etc?

---

5 THE LEARNING ACTIVITY

Links

i)   The activities link with the story through images and through themes of diversity and of anti-bullying.

ii) The assembly connects with the story through valuing differences in people.

iii) If you wish to link the activity to the assembly, one or more of the children could read their chosen poem. One of the advice role-plays could be performed. The children's drawings could be displayed in the assembly hall.

ACTIVITY SUGGESTIONS

I CHOOSING AN ACTIVITY LINKED TO THE STORY

(A) Let the children:

- Draw (or paint) an English seaside scene.

or

- From the story, draw (or paint) the hairdressing on the beach, or the aeroplane flying through clouds.

or

- Lucy's problem was solved by hair braiding. Write a story in which a problem of some kind is solved.

or

- Write a story which Ama could have told Lucy called, 'Another Tale from the Beach'.

Resources needed

Colouring pencils or paint

(B) Poetry:

- Write a poem called 'On the Beach'.

or

- Give each child a school poetry (or song) book. Ask them to find a poem (or song) which connects with the story. It could be about an aeroplane or about flying to another country. It could be about being kind to friends as Helen was. It could even be about a holiday or the seaside or even about crocodiles or hair! After some reading time, ask some of the children to read their poem (or song) and to explain its link with the story *Tales from the Beach*.

Resources needed

Poetry and/or song books

2 A DIFFERENT 'PROPER'

Contact your local authority multicultural resources centre/service for information about styles of dress from different cultural traditions. Aim to show that people dress differently around the world and that these differences are interesting and acceptable (different 'propers').

3 FOCUS ON BULLYING (HOW TO STOP BEING A BULLY)

Most people have bullied someone at least once. However, bullies pick on people all the time because it makes them feel good. They have a problem. With the children's help make a list of reasons why people might become bullies.

For example:

- they are being bullied themselves

- they are spoilt and always want their own way

- they are sad or frustrated and want others to feel bad too

- they are scared they might be bullied unless they seem 'tough'

- they are jealous of people who have more or seem happier.

With the children's help make a list of things a bully could do to stop being a bully. For example:

- if they are being bullied or badly treated or have a problem – tell an adult who will help

- make friends with a new pupil and help them

- say sorry to someone they have bullied

- give themselves a fresh start with new people by joining a club

- refuse to be part of a bullying gang.

In pairs the children could take it in turns to be an adviser as follows:

Child A: a bully who wants to stop   Child B: the adviser

Child B: a child who is being bullied   Child A: the adviser

Assembly

Theme: Empathy and Difference

Introduction

The assembly leader introduces the themes of empathy and difference. We are all different – each a unique individual with our own likes and dislikes, interests, personality, etc. We live in a world full of different ways of life, ways of dressing, etc. Rather than to fear or pick on those who look different, we should learn to be open minded and generous.

Story

Assembly leader:

'Our story today is about Lucy, a brave girl who learns, far away in another country, that to be different is just fine and that sometimes, what is not beautiful in one place, may be beautiful in another.'

The assembly leader reads the story – *Tales from the Beach*.

Poem or song

You can choose a poem or a song or both. Alternatively, you can have a child (or children) read the poems they chose or wrote in class and have one of the songs that were chosen. Select poems and songs which are relevant to the theme or which echo the story in some way.

Examples

Poems:

Haircut (unkind remarks about a short haircut)
Page 89 in *Please Mrs Butler*, by Allan Ahlberg, published by Puffin, 1984.

Clothes (fashions change giving different 'propers')
Page 119 in *A Second Poetry Book*, compiled by John Foster, published by Oxford University Press, 1980.

Songs:

Points of View (difference of perspectives)
No. 45 in *Every Colour Under the Sun*, published by Ward Lock Educational Co. Ltd, 1983.

Seeds of Kindness (kind behaviour makes us happy)
No. 42 in *Every Colour Under the Sun*, published by Ward Lock Educational Co. Ltd, 1983.

Look out for Loneliness (being kind to those who are sad or lonely)
No. 36 in *Someone's Singing Lord* (2nd Edition), published by A&C Black, 2002.

Quiet reflection or prayer

For a universal, humanistic or multi-faith assembly:

Quiet reflection

The assembly leader says:
'Close your eyes and think about how Helen has supported her friend Lucy and let us decide to be a good friend, like Helen. (Pause) Lucy was the same person with or without braids. Let us also try not to judge people by their appearance. (Pause) Finally, think how boring the world would be if we were all the same and pause to be happy that there are so many different kinds of people.' (Pause)

Or for Christian schools:

Prayer

Lord God,
Help us to be kind, thoughtful and loving to our friends, every day. Help us to be kind to new people too, and not to judge anyone by their appearance. We are grateful, Lord, for the wonderful diversity You have created – the many kinds of people and ways of life.

Amen.

A Blurry World

Teacher's Notes

Theme Two (b): Difference in Appearances

Inclusive Education: Developing an acceptance of and empathy concerning differences in appearance is part of **Inclusive Education**

We need to look beyond first impressions of people, especially when people are sensitive about their appearance, and get to know people for their personality and character.

Lesson Plan

This five-part lesson plan is only a guide. Teachers are likely to add to or amend the learning activities which are suggested and may sometimes wish to substitute their own. For any part of the session they may wish to allow more or less time than that suggested.

1 Introduce the theme *5 minutes*

Hannah wears glasses and is teased for wearing them by Yasmin. Hannah accepts that she needs glasses but realises too that she doesn't need to accept unkind comments about them.

2 Vocabulary *5 minutes*

The teacher ensures that the children understand the words given – usually within the context of the story as it is being read.

3 The story *5–10 minutes*

The teacher shows the illustration and reads the story.

4 Talking about the story *10–15 minutes*

The teacher uses some of the questions and discussion points given, stimulating the children to talk about the story/theme.

5 The learning activity *20–35 minutes*

Learning activities are suggested. One could be selected and others used in subsequent, follow-up lessons.

Total time *45–60 minutes*

1 INTRODUCE THE THEME

Key points

● We are all different in appearance, but some children may be sensitive about their own difference because it is very noticeable or what they might consider to be unattractive. Although a difference in appearance might be very common (wearing glasses, or being very thin for example), children may still be self-conscious about it and other children should be aware of this and develop empathy.

2 VOCABULARY

Use your usual methods for introducing new words.

The difficult words/references in the story are:

'thorn in the flesh'	–	*a phrase used by St Paul in the New Testament part of the Christian Bible to describe a repeated and persistent problem*
aura	–	*a distinctive quality considered to be characteristic of a person*
snubbed	–	*having 'cold-shouldered' someone, or been unkind to someone who was trying to be friendly*
sarcasm	–	*using words that are the opposite of what they say to tease or criticise*
morose	–	*gloomy or sad*
'bottle-ends'	–	*a rude phrase about someone who has thick lenses in their glasses*
mock	–	*to mimic in ridicule*
abseiling	–	*to lower oneself down a rock face using a double rope*
gloat	–	*to be pleased in an unkind way that you have done better than someone else*
cajole	–	*to coax someone to do something*
staccato	–	*short, abrupt sounds*

3 THE STORY:

A Blurry World

A Blurry World

Hannah was a cheerful soul. She had the sort of smile that was catching, and even behind her glasses her eyes smiled too. Hannah was well liked at school, but she did have one 'thorn in her flesh' (a phrase she had remembered from Sunday School) and that was Yasmin, a girl in her year who seemed to take pleasure in chipping away at Hannah's smile and confidence.

Yasmin had an 'aura' about her. Girls and boys flocked around her in equal number wanting to please her, flatter her and be liked by her. It wasn't just that she was attractive, although she certainly was that, with her long dark hair, skin the colour of coffee and penetrating brown eyes. She had a presence about her that seemed to draw people in. In a way Hannah was no exception, she wanted to be friends with her, but was constantly snubbed.

"Don't take it personally Hannah" reassured Aneela, one of Hannah's best friends. "Yasmin's lovely, but she does get moody sometimes!"

"But why is she always moody with me?" moaned Hannah, pushing up her glasses, that were sliding down her nose. "There doesn't seem to be a reason, that's what gets me."

All the talk in the playground was about the Outdoor Activity week, open to children in Year 5 and 6. A large group was going, including Hannah and Yasmin.

"Are you packed for the trip then Yasmin?" queried Hannah, in yet another effort to be friendly.

"Yes, just about. Are you coming then?" asked Yasmin, as if surprised.

"You bet, wouldn't miss it for all the chocolate in the world!"

Yasmin almost smiled, but flicked her hair to one side to disguise it and changed the subject.

"Why do you wear those glasses?" asked Yasmin, almost accusingly.

Hannah frowned with a slight look of bemusement.

"Because I need them," she said with undisguised sarcasm at such a ridiculous question.

"They make your eyes look so small, Hannah, you look like a little pig." Yasmin chuckled to herself, as if she had made a great joke.

Some other friends of Yasmin overheard and joined in the chuckling, even though some of them didn't know what they were laughing at.

Hannah was burning inside with anger and embarrassment. She didn't know which would take over: it was the embarrassment.

"I didn't choose to wear glasses, everything's a blur otherwise."

She walked away, angry with herself for not finding something cutting or witty to say in response to the unkindness.

For the rest of lunchtime Hannah huddled on a bench in the far corner of the playground away from Yasmin's penetrating stare. Hannah privately hated her glasses. She always made light of them, joked about the thickness of the lenses and tried so hard to be the uncomplaining person that everyone expected her to be. It took only the slightest reference to her glasses to send Hannah into a morose mood which was unusual for her.

The Tuesday arrived of the Outdoor Activity week, with much excitement. Various households had been carefully packing bags up the night before. Hannah's mum had been flitting about like a manic fly, always inclined to over pack.

"Mum, I'm sure that's enough T-shirts. Honestly! I'm not going to fall in the river every day!"

"Sorry love. I know I'm faffing, but keeping busy helps take my mind off how much I'll miss you. Have you got your spare glasses in?"

"Think so, they must be buried in the bottom of the bag."

Most children felt rather nervous on that Tuesday morning. Some were better at hiding it than others. Yasmin was one of the children who could hide her feelings easily. She gave her father a brief hug and then walked coolly to join her friends.

Yasmin watched as Hannah arrived. Hannah could feel Yasmin's eyes burning into the back of her neck as she hugged her mum goodbye. Hannah was also good at hiding her feelings and ran to join Aneela, carefully avoiding eye contact with Yasmin.

The next half hour was taken up with further arrivals, announcements, name checking, and bag loading before finally all the children were on the coach and "high as kites". Singing began almost immediately. All the usual songs were paraded out, including, "She'll be coming round the mountain when she comes …"

All the verses had been exhausted, but Yasmin added a new verse, looking at Hannah as she sang:

She'll be wearing bottle ends when she comes,
She'll be wearing bottle ends when she comes,
She'll be wearing bottle ends,
Wearing bottle ends,
Wearing bottle ends when she comes.

Hannah was crying inside. One of the teachers picked up on the verse but didn't realise that Hannah had been the object of Yasmin's unkindness.

"Don't like that verse Yas, leave that one out next time OK?"

There were several glasses wearers on the coach so there was no reason why Ms Scott should pick up on who Yasmin was referring to. Yasmin had a way of covering up her hostility to other children to the point where most teachers genuinely thought that Yasmin was everyone's friend.

Hannah shoved a tape into her tape player so that the remaining miles melted away without Yasmin's constant chattering and singing in the background.

Hannah was relieved to arrive at the campsite and as she stepped off the coach there was a delicious smell of greenery and vegetation.

"What a fantastic campsite!" Hannah announced to Aneela with a breathy sigh of relief.

"We are going to have some *serious* fun!!" joked Aneela.

Hannah laughed, "How can you have serious fun, you mad thing!"

"You know what I mean Han!"

Ms Scott, Mr Bennett, Mr Ridley and Miss Shah bustled into their various roles of responsibility. Ms Scott was allocating tents.

"Hannah, are you OK to share with Aneela, Emily, Yasmin and Beth?"

"Yes, that's fine Ms Scott."

Hannah's heart sank. She had not counted on sharing a tent with Yasmin.

"That's the trouble with being so easy going," thought Hannah. "No one thinks you mind anything."

"Are you and your glasses OK Han?" asked Yasmin, as she started to shift her bags into the tent.

"Please *don't* call me Han," said Hannah in a quiet but assertive voice. (Only her *best* friends called her Han.)

"I was wondering if you sleep with your glasses on so that you can see your dreams better?" Yasmin asked with mock innocence.

"You are unbelievable Yasmin, what is your problem?" Hannah didn't wait for a reply, she threw her bag angrily into the tent and ran off to find Aneela, who was helping in the kitchen tent.

Aneela took one look at her friend and excused herself quickly from the vegetable chopping.

"What's up Han?"

"It's Yasmin, going on about my glasses again."

Aneela put her arm round her friend's shoulder and looked straight into Hannah's eyes.

"Look Hannah, I'm not sure what is going on in Yasmin's head at the moment, but if this carries on, one of us will need to talk to one of the teachers about it."

Hannah burst into tears at the thought of having to involve one of the teachers.

"I *hate* my glasses," she sobbed. "They're ugly looking, they smear up, they slip off my nose, they make me look like someone that I'm not. I am sick to death of them." Hannah ripped off her glasses and threw them down.

Hannah was more upset and agitated than Aneela had ever seen her: so much for her laid-back friend.

"It's OK Hannah," Aneela said, rescuing Hannah's glasses. "Your glasses aren't that bad you know and a blurry world wouldn't be much fun, would it? Anyway, didn't you tell me your mum was going to buy you a new pair when we get back from the trip?"

Hannah continued to cry, and Aneela's shoulder became extremely soggy, but eventually her crying subsided.

Hannah looked up with a sorrowful expression, "You're right – I need my glasses so I'll just have to put up with them, but I *don't* have to put up with Yasmin's comments. If she says one more thing to me I'll have to tell Ms Scott – it's like bullying, isn't it?"

"Yep, that's just about it. Now, let's get on with the serious fun, OK?"

Hannah replaced the glasses that Aneela had been carefully cleaning whilst listening, hugged her friend and walked back to her tent to sort her bag out.

Hannah, despite the shaky start, went on to have a fantastic week. Her confidence grew by the day as she gave everything a go – canoeing, sailing, abseiling and hiking. What became noticeable was that Yasmin stopped joining in. She always came up with some excuse to avoid participating. Eventually Mr Ridley took her to one side.

"Yasmin what was the point of coming? This was a complete waste of money for your family. What's going on?" Mr Ridley had tried every trick in the book with Yasmin to cajole her into taking part; nothing had worked. He was very disappointed that Yasmin hadn't "come round".

Yasmin took one look at Mr Ridley's sympathetic face and burst into tears. She ran off to the far side of the campsite near the toilet tents.

Hannah was messing about with Aneela and Emily when she noticed Yasmin running past the back of their tent. Hannah had almost blocked out Yasmin's presence over the week and had negotiated a swap into another tent without having to explain the situation to anyone. Here, she was confronted with Yasmin in a miserable state.

It was not in Hannah's nature to gloat and although she still felt angry with Yasmin, she found that glimmers of compassion were bursting through, almost despite herself.

No one else had ventured over to see if Yasmin was alright. Did that say something in itself or was it just that no one else had noticed? With heart thudding Hannah found herself walking over to where Yasmin had dropped to the ground. From a distance all

Hannah could see was a bundle of clothing which jerked now and again with the force of the sobs.

"What's wrong Yasmin?" asked Hannah hesitantly. "That's if you want to talk to someone?"

"Why should you listen to me after what I've been saying to you?"

"We might not be the best of friends at the moment, but that doesn't mean that I want to see you crying."

At the undeserved kindness, Yasmin started to cry again.

"I – can't – see properly!" she blurted out, staccato fashion. "Everything – is – blurry!"

"You mean you need glasses?" asked Hannah, almost in disbelief.

"Yeah, probably bottle-ends, the way I'm seeing at the moment, I couldn't tell the teachers but I haven't been able to see well enough to join in. That's why Mr Ridley wanted a word with me just now."

"Oh grief Yasmin, I had no idea!"

"The world's been a bit blurry for a while now, but I managed to persuade dad not to take me to the optician after the last eye-test at school. I told him that I had had a bad headache that day and that was why I couldn't read the letters on the chart."

"Is this why you've been getting at me then? Because you are frightened of having glasses like me?"

"Suppose it is … I'm really sorry for what I've said, I shouldn't have been taking it out on you."

"It's almost a relief that there's an obvious reason, I was beginning to wonder what was wrong with me, you did make me very miserable you know."

"I *am* really sorry, please believe me."

There was a moment of quiet where both girls were lost in their own thoughts. Eventually Hannah spoke:

"Look, what we need is a trip to the optician together! My mum had promised me a new pair of specs and *you* need an eye-test … and *neither* of us will have bottle-ends!!"

With that, Yasmin and Hannah burst out laughing.

4 TALKING ABOUT THE STORY

Did the children understand?

- How is Hannah made miserable by Yasmin?

- Why was Yasmin so unkind to Hannah?

- What does Hannah do to make her activity week happier?

Points for discussion

- People may be more sensitive to their appearance than we think.

- What should we focus on when getting to know someone?

- Yasmin's persistent unkindness was a form of bullying. How should you respond if someone is persistently unkind to you or someone you know?

---

5 THE LEARNING ACTIVITY

Links

i) The activities link with the story through the focus on accepting each other's appearance and self-image.

ii) The assembly connects with the story through accepting our differences in appearance.

iii) If you wish to link the activity to the story, one or more of the children could read their chosen poem. The glasses designs and the pictures of friends could be displayed in the assembly hall.

ACTIVITY SUGGESTIONS

I CHOOSING AN ACTIVITY LINKED TO THE STORY

(A) Let the children choose one of the following:

- In pairs children take it in turns to sketch in pencil or pastels a portrait of each other.

or

- Write a description of someone in your class. Using only positive language, and without naming them, play 'Guess who?' in circle time (the teacher needs to ensure that every child is included).

or

- Write advice in list form of how to respond if someone bullies you. (This could then be compared with the school policy on bullying.)

Resources needed

Sketching pencils or pastels

(B) Poetry:

- Write a poem which is a celebration of how different we all are.

or

- Find a poem either individually or in a group which connects with the story. It could be about our differences, being kind or enjoying who we are.

Resources needed

Poetry and/or song books

2 DESIGNING GLASSES

Imagine you are a designer developing interesting spectacles for people who wear glasses. Design a pair of glasses thinking about the shape, and the colours. Try to make them as original as possible.

Resources needed

Card, felt pens

3 WHAT MAKES A GOOD FRIEND?

In a circle time discuss the qualities of a good friend. Ask the children to think about a friend they have now, or a friend that they would *like* to have. Draw a picture of the friend and write words and phrases around the edge of the picture which explain why they are a good friend.

Resources needed

Coloured pencils or felt pens

Assembly

Theme: Empathy and Difference

Introduction

The assembly leader introduces the theme. We all have differences in the way that we look. We need to learn to respect those differences and in particular be considerate and empathetic to people who may be sensitive or self-conscious about their own differences.

Story

Assembly leader:

'Our story today is about a girl called Hannah who wears glasses and is bullied by another girl called Yasmin.'

The assembly leader reads the story – *A Blurry World*.

Poem or song

You can choose a poem or a song or both. Alternatively, you can have a child (or children) read the poems they chose or wrote in class and have one of the songs that were chosen. Select poems and songs which are relevant to the theme or which echo the story in some way.

Examples

Poems:

Good Morning (self acknowledgement)
Page 14 in *Smile Please!* by Tony Bradman, published by Puffin, 1989.

Remember Me? (rising above bullying)
Page 14 in *Another Fifth Poetry Book*, compiled by John Foster, published by Oxford University Press, 1989.

Songs:

I Can Climb (self acceptance)
No. 17 in *Every Colour Under the Sun*, published by Ward Lock Educational Co. Ltd, 1983.

Every Colour Under the Sun (celebrating difference)
No. 16 in *Every Colour Under the Sun*, published by Ward Lock Educational Co. Ltd, 1983.

Seeds of Kindness (kind behaviour makes us happy)
No. 42 in *Every Colour Under the Sun*, published by Ward Lock Educational Co. Ltd, 1983.

Quiet reflection or prayer

For a universal, humanistic or multi-faith assembly:

Quiet reflection

The assembly leader says:
'Close your eyes and think for a moment about the way that you look – the things that you like and the things that you are sensitive about. (Pause) Resolve to accept your own differences and be sensitive to the differences of other people. (Pause) As you open your eyes, look around you and give your classmates and friends a smile as you accept their differences.'

Or for Christian schools:

Prayer

Dear God,
Thank you that we are all so different in the way that we look. We celebrate our differences today. Help us to accept what we look like and help us too to accept the differences in everyone around us, knowing that on the inside we are all made in Your loving image.

Amen.

The Deal

Teacher's Notes

Theme Three: (a)   Cultural Diversity (and friendship)

Inclusive Education: Multicultural education is part of **Inclusive Education**

> **Children need to learn not just to accept but to celebrate the interest and richness of cultural diversity. Children who experience cross-cultural cooperation and friendship gain learning of great value.**

Lesson Plan

This five-part lesson plan is only a guide. Teachers are likely to add to or amend the learning activities which are suggested and may sometimes wish to substitute their own. For any part of the session they may wish to allow more or less time than that suggested.

1 Introduce the theme   *5 minutes*

There are many different cultures in the world and also in Britain, which is a multicultural society. This means we benefit from variety – of languages, dress, arts, music, foods, etc.
What languages can you think of?
What kind of restaurants do we have?
What varieties of religions can you think of?

2 Vocabulary   *5 minutes*

The teacher ensures that the children understand the words given.

3 The story   *5–10 minutes*

The teacher shows the illustration and reads the story.

4 Talking about the story   *10–15 minutes*

The teacher uses some of the questions and discussion points given, stimulating the children to talk about the story/theme.

5 The learning activity   *20–25 minutes*

Learning activities are suggested. One could be selected and others used in subsequent, follow-up lessons.

Total time   *45–60 minutes*

1 INTRODUCE THE THEME

Key points

● Britain is a multicultural society in a multicultural world. Everyone benefits from approaching cultural diversity with interest and friendship, not with fear and fighting.

● Can the children identify different languages, foods (perhaps restaurants) and faiths?

2 VOCABULARY

Use your usual methods for introducing new words.

The difficult words/references in the story are:

Muslim	–	*a follower of Islam; someone who believes in the religious teachings of Muhammad*
sari	–	*a form of dress; a long length of cotton or silk worn by Indian women*
glumly	–	*gloomily; sadly*
playgroup	–	*a place where young children play and are looked after*
anxious	–	*worried*
disappointed	–	*let down*
tantalisingly	–	*teasingly*
gloomy	–	*dark*
appreciatively	–	*admiringly*
window dressing	–	*shop window display*

3 THE STORY:

The Deal

The Deal

"Weekends are rubbish without Rosie," Shazli grumbled. "They make her go. Every single week. I mean, would you want to visit your gran every single Saturday?"

"As a matter of fact," said Shazli's mum, "I would love to see your grandmother every week."

Shazli's grandmother lived far away in India.

"The trouble is, my girl, you need to make some more friends."

"The trouble is, mum, that's easier said than done. Not everyone likes us round here you know."

Shazli's parents had recently moved to Wales and they were the only Muslim family in their new neighbourhood.

"Give them time my dear," said her mum. "Just give them time to get to know us."

Shazli sighed. Feeling grumpy, she let the door bang in not quite a slam as she went outside to find something to do. She walked along the street to look into the window of the small shop on the corner. There, in the centre, was the game she had wanted for so long – a computer game, offered at half price.

"It's a brilliant game," said a voice full of longing. Shazli turned. It was Lauren, a girl from her school.

"If only I had £15," Lauren said.

"Hey, maybe we could buy it between us and take turns to have it," Shazli suggested. "I've got £8 left from my birthday. How about you?"

"Nothing," said Lauren. "Absolutely zilch. I've got a load of old books and toys I could sell at the school Table Top Sale next Saturday, but I've not even got £3 for a table."

"But I have," said Shazli, suddenly excited. "If we use £3 of my money, leaving £5, then if we sell your stuff for £10, making £15, then we …"

"Could buy it!" Lauren exclaimed.

They grinned at each other and solemnly they shook hands. It was a deal.

The following Saturday, Shazli and Lauren made their table look as attractive as possible, covering it completely with Lauren's old books and toys. It was fun deciding on the prices and sticking on the labels, and Shazli's mum draped three beautiful saris over a screen behind them. One was scarlet threaded with silver. The second was deep green with gold bands. The third was a lovely blue silk.

"You can sell them for £2 each," she said.

"But only you wear a sari mum."

"Yes," her mum agreed, "but the material is lovely and could be made into lots of nice things."

At 10.00, when the school doors were opened, everyone came piling in. Children from Shazli's and Lauren's class came over to look at their table and stayed to chat. Shazli enjoyed it. The problem was, no one bought anything.

"We'll not even make your £3 back at this rate," said Lauren, glumly.

In the end, they lowered their prices and gradually, the books began to sell. At 12.30 a tall lady came and examined the toys very carefully.

"I run a playgroup," she told them. "I'll buy all the toys for a fiver." Since there were only twelve toys, priced at 50p each, this wasn't a bad offer.

"Let's," Shazli said to Lauren. "There's only half an hour left."

Lauren agreed.

"Now we just need £4 more," said Shazli.

With many anxious glances at the big round clock, Shazli watched that final half-hour speed by. Every time someone came to their stall her hopes rose. But no one bought anything more.

"Never mind. We tried our best," she said, as they packed the leftover books and the three saris into a cardboard box. She could sense that Lauren was feeling as disappointed as she was herself.

On the way home the two girls stopped for one more look into the window of the corner shop. Tantalisingly, the game was still there.

"Maybe they would take £11 deposit," said Shazli.

"I doubt it," said Lauren. "The sale ends today. It will cost £30 again on Monday."

But they went into the shop anyway. It was long and rather gloomy. A woman stood behind the counter, which Lauren rested their box on.

"Excuse me please, but we wondered if you might be interested to buy any books or games?" Shazli said, very politely.

"Sorry kids," the woman replied, "I've no kids to buy them for, d'you see?"

But as Lauren reached for the box the woman said, "Hang on a minute, are these for sale too?" She stroked the sari material appreciatively. Shazli nodded.

"How much?" asked the woman. "Only I want to dress my shop window. Everyone's doing it. Have you noticed?"

"£2 each," said Shazli, eagerly. "But you can have all three for £4."

The woman said nothing. She continued to stroke the silky material. She seemed lost in thought.

"With the books thrown in," blurted Lauren.

The woman smiled. "Sure," she agreed. "I was just thinking about how I'll do the window."

Smiling broadly, Lauren handed over their money, and leaving the box on the table, the girls went out with their precious new game.

From outside the shop they watched as the woman did her window dressing. From a central hook at the top she draped two of the sari lengths, tying each back to frame the window as theatre curtains frame a stage. The third sari she curved, like a shiny blue river, round all the goods on display.

"Looks good," said Shazli.

"Cool," Lauren agreed.

By this time, they had become good friends. Together they walked on to Shazli's house to try out their new game. It was as brilliant as they had expected. They played it all that afternoon and, becoming more and more skilful, they played it with increasing enjoyment for many Saturdays to come.

4 TALKING ABOUT THE STORY

Did the children understand?

- Why did the girls need to make £10 at the sale when Shazli already had £8 birthday money?

- How much money did the tall playgroup lady save by paying £5 for the twelve toys?

- Why did the girls get more and more enjoyment from their game?

Points for discussion

- **Friendship**
  How do we benefit from having friends? What *other* benefits might a cross-cultural friendship bring?

- **Prejudice**
  Why did some people not like Shazli's family? Why are people sometimes prejudiced against 'other' cultural groups? (Prejudice is based on ignorance and fear. Ethnic prejudices are often picked up, uncritically, from other people and the television etc.)

5 THE LEARNING ACTIVITY

Links

i)   The activities link with the story through images and through the themes of friendship and cultural diversity.

ii) The assembly connects with the story through valuing friendship and cultural diversity.

iii) If you wish to link the activity to the assembly, you could use the children's own drawings and poems or poems/songs which they selected in class. The (class) welcome poster could also be displayed in the assembly hall.

ACTIVITY SUGGESTIONS

I CHOOSING AN ACTIVITY LINKED TO THE STORY

(A) Let the children:

- Draw (or paint) a scene from the story. It might be the two girls behind their stall or it might be the newly dressed shop window.

or

- Write a story about finding a new friend.

Resources needed

Colouring pencils or paint

(B) Poetry:

- Write a poem called 'My Friend'.

or

- Give each child a school poetry (or song) book. Ask them to find a poem (or song) which connects with the story. It could be about friendship or cultural diversity. After some reading time, ask some of the children to read their poem (or song) and to explain its link with the story *The Deal*.

Resources needed

Poetry and/or song books

2 MAKE CLASS WELCOME POSTERS FOR THE WALL

Use the two photocopiable pages provided. Each child can cut out (or copy) a selection of the languages (which say 'Welcome') to glue round the central English 'WELCOME'. You will thus have many posters for your classroom walls. (You could do this exercise with A4 or enlarged A3 photocopies.)

3 USING MONEY

Divide the children into small groups. Give each group a number of books. They should decide a price for each book, make out a label with that price displayed and arrange their book 'stall'. With one child for each group, acting as the 'shop-keeper', each of the other children should 'buy' two books – giving the correct money or receiving the correct change. The children would also be asked to work out the total value for the books on their stall.

Welcome

WHICH LANGUAGE?

Douitashimashite
(Japanese)

Bienvenue
(French)

Lütfen
(Turkish)

Aubite
(Yiddish)

Kripayaa
(Gujarati)

Foon ying
(Chinese - Cantonese)

Huan ying
(Chinese – Mandarin)

Dobro pozhalovat'
(Russian)

Hoan nghênh
(Vietnamese)

Khush amaadiid
(Urdu)

Sushri akal
(Punjabi)

Khosh aamadid
(Persian)

Assembly

Theme: Cultural Diversity and Friendship

Introduction

The assembly leader introduces the themes of cultural diversity and friendship. We live in a multicultural society and world. For example there are many different religions – Christianity, Hinduism, Islam, Sikhism, Judaism, Buddhism, etc. and many different languages (make use of the multilingual language posters). All these languages can say: 'Welcome'. In our school we welcome everyone. We want to be a friendly school.

Story

Assembly leader:

'Our story today is about a Muslim family who move to Wales. Shazli, the daughter in the family, using her initiative, makes a new friend.'

The assembly leader reads the story – *The Deal*.

Poem or song

You can choose a poem or a song or both. Alternatively, you can have a child (or children) read the poems they chose or wrote in class and have one of the songs that were chosen. Select poems and songs which are relevant to the theme or which echo the story in some way.

Examples

Poems:

I had no friends at all (making a friend)
Page 18 in *A First Poetry Book*, by Michael Rosen, published by Oxford University Press, 1979.

Swaps (not reaching a deal)
Page 34 in *Please Mrs Butler*, by Allan Ahlberg, published by Puffin, 1984.

Songs:

Working Together (people from all countries working together)
No. 37 in *Every Colour Under the Sun*, published by Ward Lock Educational Co. Ltd, 1983.

Black and White (cooperation of black people and white people: all learning together)
No. 41 in *Every Colour Under the Sun*, published by Ward Lock Educational Co. Ltd, 1983.

Quiet reflection or prayer

For a universal, humanistic or multi-faith assembly:

Quiet reflection

The assembly leader says:
'Turn your mind to the value of friendship. Why do we like to have friends? (Pause) Think how you would feel if you had no friends. (Pause) Let's decide to be kind to our friends and to be friendly and welcoming to all new children and teachers. (Pause) Turn your mind to the value of our multicultural world. We value variety and learn from difference. (Pause) Let's be friendly to everyone: black and white; Muslim and Christian; English and Welsh and Indian.' (Pause)

Or for Christian schools:

Prayer

Our Father,
Bless all our friends and all children and adults who are new to our school. Help us to make newcomers feel welcome. Thank you for our wonderful, multicultural world, and help humankind to live together in friendship and peace.

Amen.

The Boq Factor

Teacher's Notes

Theme Three: (b)   Cultural Diversity (and friendship)

Inclusive Education: Multicultural education is part of **Inclusive Education**

> Respecting and appreciating cultural diversity enables children to counteract racial prejudice and positively enjoy the differences that someone else may demonstrate in their appearance or lifestyle.

Lesson Plan

This five-part lesson plan is only a guide. Teachers are likely to add to or amend the learning activities which are suggested and may sometimes wish to substitute their own. For any part of the session they may wish to allow more or less time than that suggested.

1 Introduce the theme   *5 minutes*

Two alien cultures in outer space encounter each other unexpectedly and make negative judgements about each other based on the colour of their skin.

2 Vocabulary   *5 minutes*

The teacher ensures that the children understand the words given – usually within the context of the story as it is being read.

3 The story   *5–10 minutes*

The teacher shows the illustration and reads the story.

4 Talking about the story   *10–15 minutes*

The teacher uses some of the questions and discussion points given, stimulating the children to talk about the story/theme.

5 The learning activity   *20–25 minutes*

Learning activities are suggested. One could be selected and others used in subsequent, follow-up lessons.

Total time   *45–60 minutes*

1 INTRODUCE THE THEME

Key points

- Mutual respect for everyone should mean that children learn to celebrate differences in colour of skin. Children also need to learn to challenge racial prejudice that may be apparent around them, in ways that they feel able.

2 VOCABULARY

Use your usual methods for introducing new words.

The difficult words/references in the story are:

glossy	–	*shiny*
meteor	–	*a piece of rock or metal that moves through space*
overview	–	*a general survey*
hostility	–	*angry opposition, behaving like an enemy*
surveillance	–	*to observe; spy-like watching*
telepathic	–	*able to communicate between one mind and another, other than through the known channels of the senses*
gene pool	–	*all the genes in an interbreeding population*
offends	–	*hurts someone's feelings*
distasteful	–	*unpleasant or offensive*
distortion	–	*misshapenness or deformity*
'cuniq'	–	*an invented word for the measurement of brain density*
'quagphur'	–	*an invented word – the zerds' equivalent to sulphur*

3 THE STORY:

The Boq Factor

The Boq Factor

The Zerds were hurtling through space at the speed of light in the Zerd capsule. The crew was on high alert because the Capsule Detector System or CDS had picked up on a meteor that was heading directly towards them. Lights were flashing and alarms were buzzing. With no room for error the Zerds were on full alert. Their two heads were bobbing and their small metallic eyes were darting as they peered from one CDS screen to the next. A nanosecond later and the capsule was 'clipped' by the meteor: the CDS had misjudged the distance by one hundredth of a millimetre!

The clipping of the Zerd capsule was enough to diminish power and affect the functioning of the CDS. The capsule was vibrating violently as a result of the impact and the Emergency Functioning System came into operation. The Zerds were fighting to keep the capsule from losing speed altogether.

"Emergency landing required," announced Chief Zerd, "all Zerds attend to the Emergency Functioning System and assess landing zones. Report back in five zerdons."

The chief could overview one end of the Emergency Functioning System (or EFS for short) with one head and use the other to monitor the screens at the far end of the capsule. As each zerdon went by, the EFS was failing to pick up on any suitable zone.

"Keep zone checking, two zerdons to go."

Once again the crew was almost frantic with seeking and checking data.

Exactly two zerdons later, one crew member pressed the zone check screen.

"Safe landing zone found, all Zerds prepare for speed loss and zoning."

With complete accuracy and precision the capsule came in to land on planet Xena.

"We have no knowledge of this planet but our data suggests a life force here. All Zerds to equip themselves with Zone Pack, including hostility belt." Having briefed the crew, Chief Zerd set about coordinating the preparation for zone entry. After further screen surveillance and monitoring Chief Zerd gave the instructions to slide the capsule panel. The hostility team stood by the panel as it opened with Zerd Zappers at the ready.

The Zerds left the capsule with both heads turning 360° using their small but powerful eyes to scan the strange terrain. The landscape was lush and green; by Zerd judgements it was similar to the tropical zone on Planet Earth which they had visited once before. There was a smell of vegetation in the air and the heat was causing the blue pores on the Zerds' skin to get larger as their indigo coloured skin fought to retain the correct Zerdic temperature range. As they stood watching and waiting (for they sensed there was something to wait for), there was a rustle of vegetation immediately behind them. All Zerds had full rotation of their heads to compensate for their large and less than nimble bodies which, although strong, could not move quickly.

In a matter of moments a row of Xenas appeared, in various shades of green with a large, oddly shaped head and four antennae with a large eye attached to each.

There was what seemed like a long silence as the two groups looked at each other, trying to make sense of what was before them. Not a movement was made, nor a word uttered. Both Zerds and Xenas could communicate telepathically when necessary between their own group: this was such a time.

For the Zerds, telepathic communication involved placing one head next to the head of another Zerd. Because the Zerds had two heads, dual communication was possible. The welter of communication that followed went something like this:

I do not like this life force, they are the colour of the creatures in our land who serve us and tend our Technical Capacity.
How can a creature of any worth be green?
They can have no skill to defend themselves for they mimic the colour of their terrain.
Too true, it is the colour of our soil and we do not dirty our hands with it.
See their thin, knobbly limbs – they have no strength.
They only have one head, imagine how little intelligence they must have …

*And look at the distortion on their head! They must have a
defective gene pool.*

*But look, they have four eyes, they would seek us out too well if
we were to hide!*

That is true. If we need to attack, best to zap the eyes first.

*Of course we shall need to attack, this life force is not worthy of
our respect.*

*Why not capture them and take them to Zerd territory to join
our bonded Zerds?*

If they are the colour of our soil, let them tend it!

The Xenas' telepathic conversations involved a quivering of the
antennae which appeared to carry the many thought waves:

What are we to make of this life force?

*We should attack without delay. They are not a colour worthy of
our respect.*

*Indigo is the colour of our steaming lakes that have the stench
of quagphur.*

*Indigo is also the colour of our most beautiful flower, should we
not give them peace time?*

*But look at their two heads, they would seek to overrule us with
their superior intelligence – best not to offer them trust or
peace.*

They have no place here.

*They have eyes of such little size, their sight must be even worse
than ours, we could overpower them easily.*

*Indigo is the colour of our fears for we know there is strange-
ness in our lakes, give them no more telepathic time – they
need to go or be thrown into our lakes!*

The communication continued on each side in much the same
vein, with only occasional voices suggesting the offer of peace or
trust.

Eventually Chief Zerd and Mater Xena, the Xenas' ruler,
stood forward as was customary in inter-planetary encounters.
Only the Superior Authority on each planet could communicate
in IPV (Inter-Planetary Verbalisation).

Mater Xena spoke first:

"Name yourselves for we do not know your life force."

"We are Boqazerds, from the Zerd territories. Our capsule skimmed a meteor and is in need of Technical Assistance."

"I am Mater of the Xenaboqs, we will assist you because we wish you to leave quickly: your colour offends us."

"We have no wish to stay, for your colour is distasteful to us. Aid us and we will leave."

"Very well, I will give you a team of our best technicians to speed your departure."

The technicians got to work almost immediately with the Zerds looking on. The Zerds watched with fascination at the different ways in which the Xenas worked and they continued telepathic communication between themselves:

They work with great skill, look at the way they are lasering the capsule skin ready for repair…

At the same time Chief Zerd and Mater Xena continued their Inter-Planetary Verbalisation, if only to pass the time.

"Your Xenas work with great skill despite their brain density."

"Xenas have a high brain density of 40 cuniqs, so of course they work with great skill! Why should you be surprised?"

"You have only one head so we thought your intelligence would be low … and of course the distortion on the side of your head suggests a defective gene pool."

Mater Xena laughed out loud.

"The 'distortion' you speak of has been created by our bio-technicians to allow for the increased brain cuniqs which increase by 10 every two light years. What is *your* combined cuniq density between your two heads?" enquired Mater Xena.

"Each head contains an average of 15 cuniqs, some Zerds have up to 20 per head."

"So our cuniq brain capacity is similar!" commented Mater Xena.

"It appears so," replied Chief Zerd rather grudgingly.

"Tell me, Chief Zerd, why your life force is indigo; for us, it is the colour of destruction."

"Indigo for us is the colour of all that is finest in Zerdic zones. Indigo is the colour of life."

"Tell me, Mater Xena, why you are the colour of our soil and dust. Only our bonded life force who serve us share your colour."

"We are green because we have Boq heritage of which we are very proud!"

"Did you say *Boq?*"

"None other."

Chief Zerd's brains were racing as he tried to take in the enormity of the information he had just received. The Boqs had been the peaceful ruling race of two galaxies for 1,000 light years and they too – the Boqazerds (for that was their full name) – were of Boq descent.

Could it be that the Xenaboqs were distant relatives?

Mater Xena's brain was also racing. She had just realised the shared Boq heritage too.

"It seems we have a shared history. You may find that your bonded workers are also of Boq ancestry, have you ever asked them?"

"We communicate with them as little as possible, I told you, their colour is offensive to us. We give instructions – that is all."

"Perhaps it is time to communicate more! Perhaps you and your crew would like to stay for a number of xenacs in order that we can data-collect on each other. It seems that we have much to learn about each other's life force!"

"I shall speak to my crew, I think it unlikely that they will want to stay."

Chief Zerd turned his attention to his crew and the Xenaboqs who were assisting them. To his amazement, and defying all Universal Laws, the two life forces were communicating telepathically with great enthusiasm and mutual interest. The capsule had been repaired in a matter of zerdons and the two groups were sitting next to the capsule with thought waves flying at huge speed between each other.

"Mater Xena, I believe the decision has been made for me! We shall stay a while."

4 TALKING ABOUT THE STORY

Did the children understand?

- Who are the two groups of aliens?

- Why did the Zerds have to land on planet Xena?

- How did the aliens communicate with their own group without the other aliens hearing them?

- What is the first negative judgement that each group makes about the other?

- Why did the Zerds decide to stay?

Points for discussion

- Why is it unacceptable to make negative judgements about someone based on the colour of their skin? (We are all worthy of respect; we are all unique individuals.)

- What is prejudice based upon? (Ignorance and fear)

- How might you respond to someone who was making racist comments? (It may be appropriate for a child to challenge racist comments, but teacher support can be expected.)

5 THE LEARNING ACTIVITY

Links

i)   The activities link with the story through the focus on celebrating differences in skin colour and challenging prejudice.

ii) The assembly connects with the story through celebrating our cultural diversity including differences in skin colour.

iii) If you wish to link the story to the assembly, one or more of the children could read their chosen poem. Pictures of the aliens and/or portraits of children could be displayed in the assembly hall.

ACTIVITY SUGGESTIONS

I CHOOSING AN ACTIVITY LINKED TO THE STORY

(A) Let the children:

- Draw a picture of either a Zerd or a Xena; make sure they match the description in the story.

or

- Imagine you are a Zerd or a Xena who didn't choose to respond with prejudice. How would you greet an alien to your planet in a positive way? Describe the meeting.

Resources needed

Coloured pencils or felt pens

(B) Poetry:

- Write a poem which celebrates differences in skin colour and/or culture.

or

- In pairs or in small groups, find a poem or song which fits with the story. It could be about different cultures, peace, friendship or outer space.

2 PAINT A PICTURE OF YOURSELF OR YOUR FRIEND MIXING THE COLOURS CAREFULLY TO CREATE THE CORRECT SKIN TONE

Resources needed

Paints and paper

3 THE ZERDS EQUIPPED THEMSELVES WITH A HOSTILITY BELT.

Imagine you are a Zerd who is challenging the need for a hostility belt. Design a 'friendship belt' to be used when encountering different aliens. What would it include?

Resources needed

Card, felt pens

Assembly

Theme: Cultural Diversity

Introduction

The assembly leader introduces the theme. We live in a world of great diversity: some people fear such diversity and that fear can lead to prejudice. We need to remember that cultural diversity is a good thing and something to be celebrated.

Story

Assembly leader:

'Our story today is set in outer space and is about two groups of aliens who instead of greeting each other in friendship, make judgements about each other based primarily on skin colour.'

The assembly leader reads the story – *The Boq Factor*.

Poem or song

You can choose a poem or a song or both. Alternatively, you can have a child (or children) read the poems they chose or wrote in class and have one of the songs that were chosen. Select poems and songs which are relevant to the theme or which echo the story in some way.

Examples

Poems:

Duncan Gets Expelled (a child is expelled for colour prejudice)
Page 50 in *Two's Company*, by Jackie Kay, published by Puffin, 1994.

Ibble Obble (aliens trying to communicate – light hearted)
Page 53 in *Smile Please!* by Tony Bradman, published by Puffin, 1989.

Songs:

Shalom (about peace)
No. 76 in *Alleluya!* (2nd Edition), published by A&C Black, 1980.

Peace is Flowing like a River (a hope that virtues will flow freely in the world)
No. 48 in *Alleluya!* (2nd Edition), published by A&C Black, 1980.

Every Colour Under the Sun (celebrating differences)
No. 16 in *Every Colour Under the Sun*, published by Ward Lock Educational Co. Ltd, 1983.

Black and White (cooperation of black people and white people: all learning together)
No. 41 in *Every Colour Under the Sun*, published by Ward Lock Educational Co. Ltd, 1983.

Quiet reflection or prayer

For a universal, humanistic or multi-faith assembly:

Quiet reflection

The assembly leader says:
'Close your eyes for a moment and think of children, adults, friends or family who have a different skin colour to your own. (Pause) Be ready to show friendship and kindness to everyone, whatever culture they may come from and whatever skin colour they have. (Pause) We can replace fear with respect and kindness.' (Pause)

Or for Christian schools:

Prayer

Dear God,
You have created a world full of different cultures and people with different skin colours. Today we celebrate the diversity of Your world and the people in it. Help us to respect everyone and show kindness and friendship. There is no room for fear when Your love is in our hearts.

Amen.

One Step Ahead

Teacher's Notes

Theme Four (a)   The Differently Abled (Abilities and Disabilities)

Inclusive Education: Unlearning prejudice against the disabled is part of **Inclusive Education**

> Unless mainstream children unlearn prejudice against the disabled, integration of disabled children will be difficult. Disabled children need to be seen for who they are – beyond the labels. We all have a range of abilities and disabilities but children (people) with certain kinds of disabilities are often patronised, or excluded or bullied.

Lesson Plan

This five-part lesson plan is only a guide. Teachers are likely to add to or amend the learning activities which are suggested and may sometimes wish to substitute their own. For any part of the session they may wish to allow more or less time than that suggested.

1 Introduce the theme   *5 minutes*

The story is about a blind boy. He is an intelligent and competent boy.

2 Vocabulary   *5 minutes*

The teacher ensures that the children understand the words given.

3 The story   *5–10 minutes*

The teacher shows the illustration and reads the story.

4 Talking about the story   *10–15 minutes*

The teacher uses some of the questions and discussion points given, stimulating the children to talk about the story/theme.

5 The learning activity   *20–25 minutes*

Learning activities are suggested. One of these could be selected and others used in subsequent, follow-up lessons.

| Total time | *45–60 minutes* |

1 INTRODUCE THE THEME

Key points

● Explain the 'social model' of disability at an appropriate (Key Stage Two) level. We all have abilities and disabilities. How much our disabilities are a problem depends on the world out there. (Fog is not a handicap to a blind person but not having sounds with the pedestrian red/green lights would be.) Ask the children to give examples of a good and a bad environment for (a) a blind person (b) a person in a wheelchair.

2 VOCABULARY

Use your usual methods for introducing new words.

The difficult words/references in the story are:

rapidly	–	*quickly*
retreating	–	*going back*
coping	–	*managing*
individual	–	*a person; one thing*
tuition	–	*teaching*
conscious	–	*aware; awake; knowing what is happening*
spanned	–	*bridged; reached from one side to the other*
conga	–	*a kind of dance*
reluctantly	–	*unwillingly*
pea-souper	–	*very thick fog*
dipped	–	*curved down; downward slope*
gratitude	–	*thankfulness*

3 THE STORY:

One Step Ahead

One Step Ahead

Tom pushed open the garden gate. Its newly painted wood felt cool and smooth under his hand. As it swung inward he heard its familiar squeak but he also heard rapidly retreating footsteps down the path of the house next door. Shrugging, trying not to care, he went down his own path and into his house. A delicious smell of roasting chicken greeted him.

"Yum. Roast dinner. I'm starving," he called as he made for the kitchen where his mum was stirring gravy.

"That new boy avoided me again," he said, his face turned towards her.

"As soon as he hears my stick he shoots back inside."

"Maybe he's never met a blind boy," said his mum. "He might be a bit scared. People who can see rely on sight so much it frightens us to think of coping without it. He probably just needs to get to know you."

"Well, since he always runs off, he never will."

....

Tom awoke, happy that it was Saturday. Drum Class instead of school. But something was different. Tom listened. There was something different about the sounds from outside. That was it! There was less noise than usual – less traffic and fewer people. And what sounds there were seemed more distant, almost muffled.

"It's fog," his mum told him at breakfast. "An unusually thick fog. I'll phone to see if Drum Class is still on."

Hoping that it was, Tom listened to her side of the call.

"Hi, Mrs Birch. This is Tom's mum. Is the class on today – with this fog?"

There was a pause.

"Oh sure. The fog makes no difference to Tom."

After a second pause his mum ended the call saying,

"Good. He'll be there then. Bye."

Tom grinned, pleased.

"Mrs Birch said she's sure not everyone will turn up but she'll have to be there anyway for the few who do. The Taylor twins only live a few doors away apparently. You'll get more individual tuition today, Tom," his mum said.

The Story

She made him wear his heavy coat and gave him a woollen scarf to wrap round his nose and he set out, warm as toast.

It was a ten-minute walk to the Community Hall where the Drum Class was held. Tom walked down his cul-de-sac and along the street to the field. He met no one. It seemed that with the fog, people were staying indoors. He stepped onto the field which he must cross, conscious, as usual, that it felt softer but less even under his feet. His stick told him that he had reached the wooden bridge which spanned a small stream. He crossed this with ease, swinging his stick from one edge to the other as he walked a perfect straight line down the middle. He was so used to this crossing that he was always able to enjoy the liquid sounds of the water flowing beneath. Once he had walked through the field there was just one road to cross. Tom listened for traffic. He heard a car approaching very slowly. He waited, patiently, for it to pass.

··

Only a few local boys had turned up for their drum lesson. Tom's mum was right. Tom had extra tuition.

"You've really mastered that tricky rhythm," Mrs Birch told him. "And it's very complicated. Well done, Tom."

Tom was pleased. He loved playing the drums, and learning new pieces. It felt great to be playing with more and more skill.

"Practise hard this week," Mrs Birch told him, "and we'll try jazz tunes next Saturday."

As Tom walked home, tapping his stick on the dirt track that led through the field, his mind was on drumming, until, that is, he became aware of voices at the wooden bridge ahead.

"We can't Alex. We'll have to go back." Tom recognised the woman who had moved in next door. Unlike her son, she usually greeted Tom, and she knew his name.

"But mum, I want to go home."

"Shh. Listen. I think I can hear someone."

Tom continued to approach them. As he drew near the woman said,

"It's Tom. Hello Tom. It's Mrs Drodge here, and Alex."

"Hi Mrs Drodge. What's the problem?"

"We stayed at my mother's last night, and we want to go home. But I don't think we can go over the bridge in this fog. It doesn't have any side to hold on to. You're not planning to walk over, surely."

"The fog makes no difference to me Mrs Drodge. In fact, if Alex holds onto my waist, and you hold onto his, like in the conga, I'll take you across, easy."

There was silence.

"Are you sure it would work?" said Mrs Drodge.

"No problem. Trust me," Tom said.

He moved to the edge of the bridge.

"Come near. Watch me go over. I'll shout from the other side and then come back for you."

Before Mrs Drodge could stop him, Tom tapped his way over the bridge.

"I'm over," he called.

"Amazing," called Mrs Drodge. "Don't worry about us. You go on home, Tom. We'll go back to my mother's house."

By the time she had finished speaking, Tom was back on their side.

"Come on," he said, "like the conga."

Tom stood at the edge of the bridge and Alex quickly came and held his waist. More slowly, perhaps reluctantly, Mrs Drodge, Alex's mum, then held onto Alex. Before she could change her mind Tom walked slowly onto the bridge. He moved, as usual, in a perfect straight line. Alex and Mrs Drodge held on behind. Soon they were all safely over.

"Yes!" shouted Alex.

Tom could hear the other boy's excitement at what they had done.

"Brilliant, Tom. That was brilliant," he said.

"Thanks Tom," said Mrs Drodge.

"No problem. You're welcome," said Tom. "Come on, I'll lead us home."

He tapped his way along the street, going more slowly than usual, for the sake of Alex and Mrs Drodge who were keeping close behind him.

He heard someone coming towards them.

"Someone's coming," he warned, and they kept to one side and waited.

A man passed by.

"Real pea-souper isn't it?" he said.

Soon after this Tom's stick told him that he had reached a pavement edge, where a road went off into the avenue before their own.

"We're at Bude Avenue," he warned them, over his shoulder. "The edge is right here."

And at the other side of the road, he stopped, just ahead of them, to show where they must step back up from the road. When Tom reached the corner of their own avenue, he came close to the place where the pavement dipped quite sharply. Again his stick told him of the change of level and once more he warned his companions. "Mind the dip," he said.

Alex and Mrs Drodge followed Tom up the avenue to their gates, which were side by side.

"Thanks again, Tom," said Mrs Drodge.

Tom could hear the real gratitude in her voice.

"It was lucky for us you were there."

"I'd been to drum practice."

"D'you play drums? Cool!" said Alex. "I'd love to do that."

"Come on in. I'll teach you."

"Can I mum?" said Alex, eagerly.

"Let's see what Tom's mum says," she said.

Tom led the way down his path. He knew what his mum would say.

"Sure. Come in for a coffee," she said to Mrs Drodge, "while they drum down in the basement. It's soundproof, thank goodness." Tom smiled as his mum laughed, and he led Alex down to the drums, remembering to switch the light on at the top of the stairs.

Tom enjoyed the next hour, playing for Alex and showing him how to drum. And over the next few months, he taught Alex to play. At Christmas Alex got his own drums and joined Tom's Saturday drum class. He was really keen and soon became a very good player. He was never quite as good as Tom though. Enjoying the friendly competition, Tom kept one step ahead.

TALKING ABOUT THE STORY

Did the children understand?

- Why might the new boy be a bit scared of Tom?

- How did the fog make the sounds different?

- Why didn't Mrs Birch cancel Drum Class?

- How did Tom get Alex and Mrs Drodge safely across the bridge?

- Why did Tom switch on the light at the top of the stairs?

Points for discussion

- **Learning through the senses**
  If we had no sight, sound, touch, smell or taste we could learn nothing about the world. The senses are the means through which we learn.
  How did Tom learn about the world? How do we know he was an intelligent boy?

- **Who was disabled by the fog?**
  Try to convey the idea of our abilities and disabilities interacting with the world outside, i.e. with our environment. We can be disabled in one respect (e.g. sight) and not in another (e.g. reasoning, memory, etc.).

- **We all have abilities**
  Tom was good at drumming. What are you good at? (This provides an opportunity to build the children's self-esteem.) The teacher should join in – pointing out what less able or less self-confident children are good at – perhaps those who have not spoken up for themselves.

 # THE LEARNING ACTIVITY

Links

i) The activities link with the story through the theme of abilities and through some focus on the senses.

ii) The assembly connects with the story through valuing the senses, including sight, while also valuing everyone's abilities.

iii) If you wish to link the activity to the assembly, you could use the children's poems and drawings. One or more of the children could read their chosen poem to the class. Some drum music could be played.

ACTIVITY SUGGESTIONS

I CHOOSING AN ACTIVITY LINKED TO THE STORY

(A) Let the children:

- Draw (or paint) Tom playing the drums or Tom leading Alex and Mrs Drodge across the bridge. (How can you represent the swirling fog?)

or

- Write a story called 'One Foggy Day'.

or

- Write a story about a disabled child who has an adventure.

Resources needed

Colouring pencils or paint

(B) Poetry:

- Write a poem called 'Sounds'.

or

- Give each child a school poetry (or song) book. Ask them to find a poem (or song) which connects with the story. It could be about skills, sights, sounds, music, drums or fog. After some reading time, ask some of the children to read their poem (or song) and to explain the link with the story *One Step Ahead*.

Resources needed

Poetry and/or song books

2 DRUMS

Select a piece of music which the children will like and which features some form of drumming (e.g. steel pan, timpani (kettle drums), Djembe, Taiko or Tabla). Enjoy listening to this with the children – beating out the drum rhythm.

3 A LINK PROJECT

Many mainstream and special schools have benefited from a link scheme. (Link schemes consist of a project undertaken in common by children from both schools. Children visit the 'other' school in conducting the project. Both sets of children are learning and cooperating. The mainstream children benefit from getting to know disabled children as real people. The special school children benefit from becoming part of the mainstream.) If your school is already involved with a link project, you could perhaps make use of the story in connection with the project. If your school is not involved with a link project, perhaps your class could pioneer such a link with a special school.

Assembly

Theme: Abilities and the Senses

Introduction

The assembly leader introduces the themes of abilities and senses. Disabled children are not different. We all have abilities and disabilities. We should appreciate everyone for who they are. We should also appreciate our senses – of sight, sound, taste and smell, and be grateful if we have them all.

Story

Assembly leader:

'Our story today is about Tom, a blind boy with many abilities. He helps the new boy next door in a rather unusual way.'

The assembly leader reads the story – *One Step Ahead*.

Poem or song

You can choose a poem or a song or both. Alternatively, you can have a child (or children) read the poems they chose or wrote in class and have one of the songs that were chosen. Select poems and songs which are relevant to the theme or which echo the story in some way.

Examples

Poems:

Sounds in the Evening (learning through sounds)
Page 18 in *A First Poetry Book*, by Michael Rosen, published by Oxford University Press, 1979.

Chips (taste and texture)
By Cook: Page 69 in *A Second Poetry Book*, compiled by John Foster, published by Oxford University Press, 1980.

By Holder: Page 48 in *A Very First Poetry Book*, compiled by John Foster, published by Oxford University Press, 1984.

Flashlight (used like Tom uses his stick)
Page 16 in *A First Poetry Book*, by Michael Rosen, published by Oxford University Press, 1979.

Songs:

Music of the World a-Turnin (hearing the beauty of sound)
No. 19 in *Alleluya!* (2nd Edition), published by A&C Black, 1980.

Use Your Eyes (celebration of seeing and hearing)
No. 11 in *Every Colour Under the Sun*, published by Ward Lock Educational Co. Ltd, 1983.

I Love the Sun (God made us all, experiencing His world)
No. 12 in *Someone's Singing Lord* (2nd Edition), published by A&C Black, 2002.

Give to us Eyes (using our eyes, ears and hands)
No. 18 in *Someone's Singing Lord* (2nd Edition), published by A&C Black, 2002.

Quiet reflection or prayer

For a universal, humanistic or multi-faith assembly:

Quiet reflection

The assembly leader says:
'Imagine you are outside on a hot summer day. What can you see, and hear and feel and smell? (Pause) Let us be grateful for all our senses and use them to enjoy and learn about the world. (Pause) Let us decide to be helpful to anyone who cannot see or hear or walk, while recognising that there are many things which they can do.' (Pause)

Or for Christian schools:

Prayer

Dear God,
Thank you for the wonderful and beautiful world. Open our eyes and ears to really see and hear it. Give us the understanding and wisdom to be helpful to those whose senses are impaired, while seeing everyone as the valuable and able person they are.

Amen.

All of a Puzzle
Teacher's Notes

Theme Four (b)	The Differently Abled (Abilities and Disabilities)
Inclusive Education:	Unlearning prejudice against the disabled is part of **Inclusive Education**

> Disabled children are often misjudged. Children need to learn to accept people's impairments and not make assumptions about what a disabled child can or can't do. Disabled children are as individual as 'ordinary' children.

Lesson Plan

This five-part lesson plan is only a guide. Teachers are likely to add to or amend the learning activities which are suggested and may sometimes wish to substitute their own. For any part of the session they may wish to allow more or less time than that suggested.

1 Introduce the theme *5 minutes*

A boy joins a scout group and demonstrates behaviour that is considered 'different', but he has abilities which are not initially realised.

2 Vocabulary *5 minutes*

The teacher ensures that the children understand the words given – usually within the context of the story as it is being read.

3 The story *5–10 minutes*

The teacher reads the story and shows the illustration.

4 Talking about the story *10–15 minutes*

The teacher uses some of the questions and discussion points given, stimulating the children to talk about the story/theme.

5 The learning activity *20–25 minutes*

Learning activities are suggested. One could be selected and others used in subsequent, follow-up lessons.

Total time	*45–60 minutes*

1 INTRODUCE THE THEME

Key points

● Children with a learning disability can be misjudged for their mental abilities. Children with ASD (Autistic Spectrum Disorder) may demonstrate different behaviour – but there is a spectrum of abilities as well as disabilities. It is important that children respect the differences of learning disabled children and see them as individuals.

2 VOCABULARY

Use your usual methods for introducing new words.

The difficult words/references in the story are:

volleyball	–	*a game in which two teams hit a large ball to and fro over a net with their hands*
vicious	–	*cruel and aggressive*
instilled	–	*infused slowly into the mind*
'whooped and hollered'	–	*shouted out in an excited way*
'turbo-charged'	–	*a turbine, operated by the exhaust gases of an engine, which boosts its power*

3 THE STORY:

All of a Puzzle

All of a Puzzle

I get a lot of stick for being in the Scouts, but it doesn't matter to me. All my friends can't understand why I don't want to be in the Guides, but I don't understand why they do! My best friend thinks it's because I like one of the boys. What's wrong with liking boys' company? Do we all have to be the same?

Anyway, with three brothers I spend more time with boys than girls: I'm sort of used to it I suppose.

Scouts has been going great the last few months: Steve the Scout leader is brilliant and another girl, called Becky, has joined – so I don't stick out like a sore thumb! Steve has introduced volley-ball and even coaches us a bit. We have a summer camp planned and there's talk of a sponsored event soon to raise some money for a new floor (marked out with a volleyball court of course!).

Out of the blue last week this new boy arrived – Jay. When I say 'arrived' I should say 'exploded' into the hall. The boy raced in as if he were being chased by killer bees. The boy's dad just about 'caught' him before he collided with the stack of chairs at the side of the hall. Steve, to my surprise, looked totally cool about it; he's usually strict with us when we get out of hand. Steve tried to welcome Jay, but Jay's eyes were everywhere, as if he was trying to make sense of another planet. As soon as his dad let go, Jay shot away and swooped round the hall making aeroplane noises. Steve walked over to where the rest of us were gathered and raised his voice above the background noises.

"Hi everybody! Good to see you all tonight. Just before you give me your subs I'd like you to meet Jay who is joining us in the Scout troop … Jay are you going to say hello?"

Jay's dad ran to 'catch' Jay again and gently brought him to where we were sitting.

"Will you say hello, Jay?" urged his dad.

Although Jay wouldn't say hello he did beam a smile in the general direction of us Scouts.

"Well the smile will do for a hello Jay! Now let me intro-duce Jay's father Anil who will be helping out each week."

"Jay looks a bit of a weird case," remarked Danny under his breath. "No wonder his dad is helping out … he'll need to keep his 'wild' son under control."

The Story

I felt Danny was being unkind but I knew what he was getting at. Jay certainly wasn't behaving normally.

"OK everyone, introductions over – let me have your subs and then we'll have a game of volleyball to start off the evening. Abi and Becky, make sure you are on separate teams – we can't have all that 'girl' power on just the one team!!"

The volleyball was great fun and initially Jay stood in position, but as soon as the ball went into play Jay ran to the door and crouched down as if he were hiding from a vicious monster. Anil sat next to his son and in between points, I could hear the reassurance that was being offered to him.

"What patience!" I thought to myself. "Every day must be a struggle to do the most ordinary of things."

The rest of the evening passed uneventfully with Jay not moving from his spot until his dad persuaded him gently to join us for the notices at the end of the session.

"Just a quick word before you go. I said I'd let you know about the sponsored event. We've had lots of sporting events in previous years – so this year we're going to have a sponsored puzzle evening; we'll call it a 'Jigathon'. Something a bit different."

There was a mixture of groans and cheers, depending on everyone's interest, but above all that, Jay's voice could be heard as he chanted "puzzle, puzzle, puzzle".

"Have we struck on a hit with Jay, Anil?"

"You could say that Steve!"

"Right listen! If you want to take part, take a form as you leave. People can sponsor you for every 15 minutes that you participate and there will be a special prize for anyone who manages to complete the baked bean puzzle! … If you haven't seen it it's a 500 piece jigsaw with nothing but baked beans on the picture!! It's a bit of a challenge to say the least!"

Jay's dad took a form as he left.

"Perhaps Anil's going to do the puzzles for Jay," commented Danny. "Can't see how Jay would stay still long enough to even pick up a piece of puzzle."

"You've been twittering in my ear all evening Danny. Why don't you give Jay a chance?" I responded.

I don't know why I was defending Jay except that my mum had instilled in me the idea that there is more to everyone than meets the eye. I could hear my mum's words even as I stood there next to Danny:

"Abi, don't be too quick to judge people and always look for the good in them if you can."

I remembered this bit of a conversation I had with mum when Grandpa was making my life miserable.

"Dig deeper with people and sometimes you'll find treasure Abi."

I *think* I knew what mum meant by this and when I was feeling patient and sat with Grandpa for a while his face would 'soften' and he would start smiling as he told me a story from his own childhood. Those stories were a bit like his 'treasure' I suppose.

Scouts was great fun the following week. Jay actually 'joined in' with the volleyball by darting around wildly and occasionally punching the ball. He had us all in stitches as he whooped and hollered. Anil looked pleased and maybe even a little bit proud that his son was joining in. At the end of the evening I felt confident enough to ask Jay to sit down next to me for the notices.

"Come and sit down Jay," I said encouragingly.

Although Jay wouldn't look at me (he always looked as if a part of him was somewhere else), he sat down really calmly. He plucked at my trainers but that was OK.

"Right then," began Steve, "the sponsored puzzle event – our Jigathon – is next week."

At the word 'puzzles' Jay started rocking and chuckling with delight.

"Puzzles, puzzles, I like puzzles."

Danny looked at me and raised his eyes to the ceiling. Danny didn't seem bothered about other people's treasure. He really seemed uncomfortable with Jay's 'unusual' behaviour.

"Glad you're showing such enthusiasm Jay! Who has their sponsor form with them?"

There was a flurry of paper as forms were eagerly passed to Steve.

Anil passed Jay his form.

"Give the form to Steve, Jay, look!"

Jay no more than glanced up, but Steve reached right across for the form to make it easier for him. Jay flapped the piece of paper but eventually released it into Steve's hand. Somehow I sensed that there had been a sense of achievement in that one simple task.

"Wow, you've done well Jay! You must be planning on having a go at quite a few puzzles next week."

Jay started to giggle. He really couldn't wait.

No one could doubt Jay's enthusiasm as he blasted into the Scout hall the following week. Whilst everyone else was carefully deciding which puzzle to 'attack' first, Jay was 'in there' with the baked bean jigsaw.

"He looks turbo-charged and he hasn't even eaten any baked beans!" joked Steve to Anil.

"I know, it's so funny, he has a whole cupboard full at home. It's the only time he stays still!"

The relative calmness of the evening was broken up with the occasional darting of Jay from one table to the next. He was, in his own way, very focused.

"No worries about his concentration this evening," commented Steve.

"Oh no, no, no. He'll be back to the baked bean puzzle if I know my son," said Anil.

In the last ten minutes of the evening, Jay and I were trying to finish the baked bean puzzle. No one else could face it, despite the promise of a prize. Jay seemed to have an imprint in his head of the puzzle piece shapes and worked with amazing speed. He finished the puzzle with five minutes to spare with token help from me.

"Fantastic Jay! Well done!" shouted Steve.

As all the Scouts started clapping, Jay started to applaud himself.

"Well with the mood you're in, it's a good job the prize is four free tickets to 'Treasure Island Adventure Park'. You can burn some energy off there with your family."

Two weeks later, having had a chance to collect our sponsor money, we discovered that Jay had raised the highest total amount.

We had enough funds not only for a new floor, but a new volleyball net and a few spare pounds to put several puzzles in the storeroom for Jay when he wanted!

4 TALKING ABOUT THE STORY

Did the children understand?

- Why does Abi prefer to be in the Scouts?

- What was unusual about the way in which Jay came into the hall?

- What is mum referring to when she talks about 'digging for treasure' with people?

- Why do you think some children thought that Jay would not be able to participate in the sponsored puzzle event?

Points for discussion

- Jay was welcomed into the Scout group by Steve. How might you welcome a child who had a learning disability?

- Was Steve right to make allowances for Jay's 'unusual' behaviour?

- When have you been surprised by abilities that you or a friend had that you weren't aware of?

5 THE LEARNING ACTIVITY

Links

i)   The activities link with the story through the focus on celebrating abilities.

ii) The assembly connects with the story through acknowledging that we all have abilities however hidden or surprising they might be.

iii) If you wish to link the activity to the assembly, one or more of the children could read aloud their chosen poem. Children could share information about clubs and organisations in the area.

ACTIVITY SUGGESTIONS

(A) Let the children:

● Draw a picture of your favourite part of the story. (You could then turn your picture into a jigsaw puzzle by sticking it onto card and drawing the puzzle pieces on the back before cutting out.)

or

● Write another chapter of *All of a Puzzle*, where Jay is included even more by the children as they get to know him better and he feels more settled in the group.

Resources needed

Coloured pencils or felt pens, card, scissors

(B) Poetry:

● Write a poem about something that you are good at.

or

● In pairs or small groups, find a poem which connects with the story. It might be about disability, talents or games.

In a circle time ask the children to talk about clubs or organisations that they belong to. Why do they enjoy it? What sort of activities do they do? Perhaps children could bring in information for their classmates if they are interested.

The children could set up their own 'Jigathon' on a small scale in the classroom, bringing in jigsaw puzzles from home.

Assembly

Theme: The Differently Abled

Introduction

The assembly leader introduces the theme. Everyone has abilities and strengths, including those with a learning disability. We should look for and celebrate the abilities of each person.

Story

Assembly leader:

'Our story today is about a boy called Jay who has abilities that are a surprise to his scout group.'

The assembly leader reads the story – *All of a Puzzle*.

Poem or song

You can choose a poem or a song or both. Alternatively, you can have a child (or children) read the poems they chose or wrote in class and have one of the songs that were chosen. Select poems and songs which are relevant to the theme or which echo the story in some way.

Examples

Poems:

Faisal (having different abilities)
Page 14 in *Poems about You and Me: A collection of poems about values*, compiled by Brian Moses, published by Wayland Publishers, 1998.

Two Carla Johnsons (accepting the different parts of ourselves)
Page 11 in *Two's Company*, by Jackie Kay, published by Puffin, 1994.

Songs:

This Little Light of Mine (letting the 'light' of each individual shine in the world)
No. 14 in *Alleluya!* (2nd Edition), published by A&C Black, 1980.

Don't You Think We're Lucky? (appreciating all the things that we learn to do)
No. 25 in *Every Colour Under the Sun*, published by Ward Lock Educational Co. Ltd, 1983.

Quiet reflection or prayer

For a universal, humanistic or multi-faith assembly:

Quiet reflection

The assembly leader says:
'Close your eyes for a moment and think of your own abilities. Are you good at being a friend? Are you good at running? Are you a good helper or organiser? Are you good at maths? (Pause) Now think of one person in your class and their abilities. (Pause) Be grateful that we all have things that we are good at.' (Pause)

Or for Christian schools:

Prayer

Dear God,
We all have 'treasure' inside us – abilities that we can be proud of. Help us to be honest about our own abilities and always look for that 'treasure' in others.

Amen.

Ten Lengths of Chocolate

Teacher's Notes

Theme Five (a)   Hidden Disability (and self-confidence)

Inclusive Education: Catering for all needs, even those that are less obvious, and helping all children to develop their self-confidence is part of **Inclusive Education**

> If we feel good about ourselves, we tend to be more understanding about the problems of other people. Developing the children's self-confidence and self-esteem, alongside their sympathy/empathy for others, is, therefore, part of developing their social skills.

Lesson Plan

This five-part lesson plan is only a guide. Teachers are likely to add to or amend the learning activities which are suggested and may sometimes wish to substitute their own. For any part of the session they may wish to allow more or less time than that suggested.

1 Introduce the theme   *5 minutes*

The story is about Jack, a boy with diabetes, and his friend Jimbo. Dan's self-confidence and Jimbo's friendship help to turn off school bullying.

2 Vocabulary   *5 minutes*

The teacher ensures that the children understand the words given.

3 The story   *5–10 minutes*

The teacher shows the illustration and reads the story.

4 Talking about the story   *10–15 minutes*

The teacher uses some of the questions and discussion points given, stimulating the children to talk about the story/theme.

5 The learning activity   *20–25 minutes*

Learning activities are suggested. One could be selected and others used in subsequent, follow-up lessons.

Total time | *45–60 minutes*

1 INTRODUCE THE THEME

Key points

- Self-confidence
  What is self-confidence? (Feeling good about yourself. Able to say what you want or need or feel. Willing to try things – even to fail and still feel OK.) Give some examples of self-confident behaviour and get the children to give some.

- Self-confidence and bullying
  People often bully if they feel insecure and if you feel insecure you may get bullied. Self-confidence helps us not to bully or to be bullied.

- Diabetes
  There are two types of diabetes – type 1 and type 2, and many people have one of them. Some people with diabetes are children and some people develop diabetes when they are grown up. Diabetes is when a person's body has either no insulin or too little insulin to convert the glucose (sugar) in the blood into energy. Having too much glucose in the blood is bad for our health. The person with diabetes may therefore be given extra insulin and also may eat less sugar. We use up more glucose through exercise. For everyone, whether they have diabetes or not, healthy eating and exercise help to keep us fit. In fact, healthy eating and exercise may help you not to develop type 2 diabetes when you are older.

2 VOCABULARY

Use your usual methods for introducing new words.

The difficult words/references in the story are:

glossy	–	*shiny*
junkie	–	*drug addict*
spurt	–	*sudden increase (e.g. of speed)*
glanced	–	*gave a quick look*
organiser	–	*the one who arranged an event*
perched	–	*half sat; sat on a small space*
popular	–	*well liked by everyone*
furious	–	*angry*
savouring	–	*enjoying*
emerged	–	*came out*
curious	–	*wanting to know*

3 THE STORY:

Ten Lengths of Chocolate

Ten Lengths of Chocolate

"**Y**ou a junkie or what?"

Jack glanced up.

"Nope," he said, and he continued to inject something into his leg. He usually liked to do this in the school sick room, but, to his surprise, today he had found it locked. It was a wet play-time, so he had then found the quietest corner of the gym, though even here, Nails Cheetham and Jimbo Hughes were perched on a small pile of rubber mats.

"It's insulin, I have diabetes," he explained, though he knew that his new class had been told this already.

"Does it hurt?" Jimbo asked.

"Not really. I'm used to it. Have to do it every day see?"

"That's brave," said Jimbo. "I hate needles."

"Hate needles!" scoffed Nails Cheetham. "You big soft sissy. You and your new junkie mate."

"Idiot!" called Jimbo as Nails went off, whistling.

"Just ignorant," Jack said, smiling.

After that, Nails always called Jack 'the junkie' and some of the other boys started to copy him.

Jack could see that it made Jimbo furious, though somehow he wasn't upset himself. He just smiled and shook his head. He had noticed that Nails, whose real name was Alan, liked all the boys to have a nickname.

One day Mrs Preston, their teacher, heard Nails.

"Now listen everyone," she said. "As I've explained already, Jack's body has stopped making insulin. That's why he has the injections. So, no more silly names please."

But whenever she wasn't there, Nails and the others continued to call Jack, 'the junkie'. Jack continued to shrug it off.

One Saturday morning, Jimbo saw Jack at the local swimming baths.

"Hi mate," he said.

"Hi Jimbo," Jack replied. "I'm practising my diving today. I want to try from the top board later."

"Wow," said Jimbo. "That's high!"

The two boys practised diving from the low board first and then from the middle one.

"Now for the top," said Jack. "Coming Jimbo? You don't have to though mate."

But Jimbo followed Jack up and watched admiringly as he did his first graceful dive from the top.

Jimbo took Jack's place at the end of the diving board. He looked down at the water. It seemed a long way below. He felt a bit scared but he took a deep breath and dived. As his body straightened, he pointed his arms down to the pool and entered the water smoothly – no belly flop of pain. He emerged, shaking the water from his eyes and grinning broadly. He saw that Jack was grinning too.

"Race you ten lengths, Jack," he said, feeling a surge of energy and joy.

The two boys swam up and down the length of the baths. Jack was soon well in the lead. Later, when they were dressed, he handed Jimbo a chocolate bar and ate one himself. Jimbo could see that he was savouring every bite.

"My mum said people with diabetes can't eat sugary things Jack," he said, curious.

"Usually," said Jack. "But after swimming my glucose is low and I can have something sweet. Ten lengths for a chocolate bar. Great! That's one reason I come swimming such a lot!"

"And that's how you've got so good at it," said Jimbo. He had seen that Jack swam like a seal – sleek and fast with a strong over-arm stroke that powered him through the water.

After that first time, the boys met up to swim most Saturday mornings, and became good friends.

About one month after the day of that first top dive, the whole class was back at the swimming baths. They were competing with other city schools for the Silverfish Swimming Trophy. Nails, who was a good swimmer and their school's swimming captain, always picked the swimmers for their school team. "Jack's brilliant," Jimbo told him, but Nails ignored this. As always, he chose his mates. By the final race, an over-arm singles race of ten lengths, their school was four points behind. The winner of the race would win five straight points. Therefore, the school that would win the coveted silver trophy, which was in the shape of a curving, gleaming fish, depended this year on who won this race.

Nails chose Buzz Bailey to swim for their school.

"I don't feel too good mate," Buzz said.

Jimbo noticed that Buzz looked a bit pale and kept rubbing his tummy.

"Jack could win it," Jimbo said. He saw that once again Nails was ignoring him.

"Miss," he said urgently to Mrs Preston, "Jack could win it."

Mrs Preston turned to Jack.

"Do you want to have a go Jack?" she said.

Jimbo felt pleased when he saw his friend nod, and he waited with some anxiety as Jack rushed off to change, reappearing in his swimming trunks, to stand at their lane, just in time.

The starting whistle blew and Jimbo watched as Jack did one of his straight shallow dives into an easy lead. Excited, Jimbo cheered with the rest of the class as Jack powered his way up and down the ten lengths, winning the race and beating the record of the fastest previous winner.

"It wasn't like in a movie," Jimbo told his dad later. "It wasn't neck and neck until a final spurt at the end. Jack was way ahead from beginning to end. We knew he was going to win from the start. Easy-peasy. It was still dead exciting though."

At speech day, because he had helped to win it, Mrs Preston chose Jack to go on the stage to receive the Swimming Trophy from the organiser of the City School swimming competition. As Jack took the trophy and shook hands with the organiser man, Jimbo clapped so hard that his hands hurt. He was proud of his friend, and, suddenly, he had an idea. After that Speech Day, he began to call Jack, 'Trophy' and, sure enough, everyone else started doing the same. The nickname stuck and was soon taken for granted. In fact, though Jack had been in Jimbo's class for only a term, he had become the most popular boy in the school. One thing didn't change though. Trophy never changed his best friend. His best friend was always Jimbo.

4 TALKING ABOUT THE STORY

Did the children understand?

- Why did Jack have to do his injection in the school gym?

- Why had Jack got so good at swimming?

- Why did Jack's race win the county swimming competition?

- How did Jack come to be known as 'Trophy'?

Points for discussion:

- **Deflecting bullying** (like Jack)
  What responses discourage bullying? (Ignoring name-calling. Avoiding bullies and making other friends. Developing your skills and self-confidence.) How can you learn to be more assertive?

- **Helping your own fitness** (like Jack)
  Discuss the importance of exercise and of healthy eating. (Less sugar and fat. More fruit and vegetables, fibre.)

5 THE LEARNING ACTIVITY

Links

i)   The activities link with the story through the children's focus on assertiveness and health.

ii) The assembly connects with the story through valuing self-confidence and fitness.

iii) If you wish to link the activity to the assembly, make use of the children's own poems, stories and pictures and also of those they chose. You could also invite a qualified speaker, such as a children's diabetes specialist nurse, to talk to the children – perhaps about how to prevent a child with diabetes from having a hypo (low blood glucose level).

ACTIVITY SUGGESTIONS

(A) Let the children:

- Draw (or paint) Jack winning the race (how do you draw/paint the water?) or receiving the trophy (how do you make it gleam like silver?).

or

- Write a story about stopping a bully.

Resources needed

Colouring pencils or paint

(B) Poetry:

- Write a poem about swimming or about some kind of race.

or

- Give each child a school poetry (or song) book. Ask them to find a poem (or song) which connects with the story. It could be about swimming, racing, fitness, exercise or about skills or self-confidence or about friendship.

Resources needed

Poetry and/or song books

There are four parts to this activity.

i)   Ask the children to make a list of:

    (a) things they are good at
    (b) things they like about themselves
    (c) good things which they have done (this is a private list).

ii) Making friends
    In pairs (the teacher should arrange these) ask the children to think about how we make friends.

    (a) what to do
    (b) what not to do.

(These ideas could then be shared with the whole class) – for example:

What to do	What not to do
show an interest	don't be insulting
smile	don't be bossy
laugh at their jokes	don't only talk about yourself
say something nice (a	don't only do the things
genuine compliment)	you want to do

iii) Dealing with insults

Arrange the pair groups into groups of four children. Ask the groups to think of four ways of dealing with insults. (These ideas could then be shared with the whole class) – for example:

- ignore the insult as though you don't care
- make a joke in response
- just smile and carry on with what you are doing
- walk away.

iv) Saying 'No'

With the whole class together, perhaps back in a circle, discuss ways of saying 'no' (in a quietly confident way) to the following:

(a) Can I copy your work?
(No. The teacher can tell and we'll both be in trouble.)
(b) Can I borrow your trainers?
(No. Sorry.)
(c) Lend me some money.
(No. I only have my dinner money.)
(d) Give us some of your sweets.
(Sorry. They've all gone.
Sorry. I licked some of them.)
(e) You've pinched my book. Let me look in your bag.
(No I haven't. Let's get the teacher to check.)

The teacher and the children can make up other requests/demands and good replies.

3 UNDERSTANDING DIABETES

Diabetes mellitus is a common condition in which the amount of glucose (sugar) in the blood is too high because the body is unable to use it properly. This is because the body's way of converting glucose into energy is not working as it should.

Normally a hormone (a chemical messenger) called insulin carefully controls the amount of glucose in your blood. Insulin is made by a gland called the pancreas which lies just behind the stomach. Glucose from food gives your body energy. Insulin acts as the 'key' to the 'lock' in cells that need this glucose. The cells use glucose as fuel for your body.

There are two types of diabetes – type 1 and type 2. People with type 2 diabetes still have some insulin producing cells, and they often only need to take tablets to help their bodies use this insulin better. People with type 1 diabetes have no insulin producing cells. This means their body no longer produces insulin, so it must be injected into them.

NB: Diabetes UK provide a leaflet called 'Children with diabetes at school. What all staff need to know.' Teachers (and parents) can order copies of the school pack by calling 0800 585 088. The pack is free. Quote code number 6001.

i)   Pass on some information, as appropriate, to the children. Some key questions could then be:

What is diabetes?
How many types of diabetes are there?
How is type 1 treated?
How is type 2 treated?

ii)   Remind children that we all need to keep fit with a healthy diet and exercise – as Steve Redgrave does. Though he has diabetes he has won an Olympic Gold Medal *five* times.

iii) Use the opportunity for some work on healthy eating – the main food groups and the right proportions we should eat of each. You can photocopy the charts for the children.

NB: The Diabetes UK Careline is open between 9 am and 5 pm Monday to Friday. Tel: 020 7424 1030. Their address is 10 Parkway, London, NW1 7AA. There is also the Diabetes UK website: www.diabetes.org.uk

A balanced diet must consist of the following

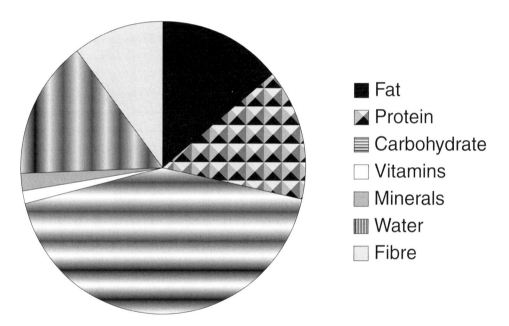

- ■ Fat
- ▨ Protein
- ▤ Carbohydrate
- ☐ Vitamins
- ▨ Minerals
- ▥ Water
- ▨ Fibre

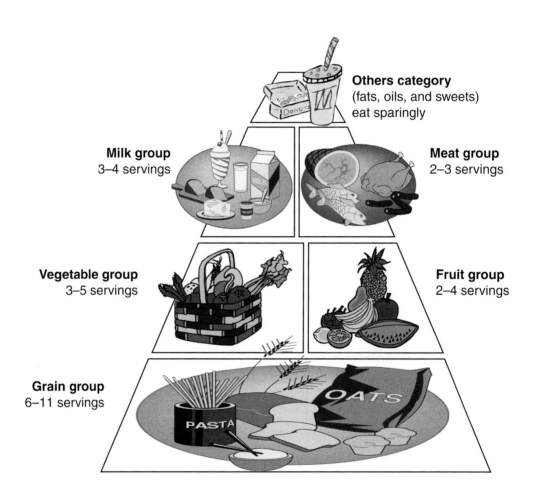

Others category
(fats, oils, and sweets)
eat sparingly

Milk group
3–4 servings

Meat group
2–3 servings

Vegetable group
3–5 servings

Fruit group
2–4 servings

Grain group
6–11 servings

© RoutledgeFalmer 2004

Assembly

Theme: Self-confidence and Fitness

Introduction

The assembly leader introduces the themes of self-confidence and fitness. It is good to feel self-confident – to like who we are. It also helps us to be confident if we keep fit and healthy through exercise and a balanced diet.

Story

Assembly leader:

'Our story today is about Jack, a diabetic boy who kept very fit through swimming. He is a self-confident boy who knows how to deal with being called a bad name.'

The assembly leader reads the story – *Ten Lengths of Chocolate.*

Poem or song

You can choose a poem or a song or both. Alternatively, you can have a child (or children) read the poems they chose or wrote in class and have one of the songs that were chosen. Select poems and songs which are relevant to the theme or which echo the story in some way.

Examples

Poems:

The Name Game (good and bad nick-names)
Page 88 in *Smile Please!* by Tony Bradman, published by Puffin, 1989.

No Swimming in the Town (an amusing poem about a closed swimming pool)
Page 77 in *A First Poetry Book*, by Michael Rosen, published by Oxford University Press, 1979.

Songs:

Getting Angry (don't say unkind things)
No. 46 in *Every Colour Under the Sun*, published by Ward Lock Educational Co. Ltd, 1983.

Do Your Best (trying is more important than winning)
No. 48 in *Every Colour Under the Sun*, published by Ward Lock Educational Co. Ltd, 1983.

I Love the Sun (using our senses)
No. 12 in *Someone's Singing Lord* (2nd Edition), published by A&C Black, 2002.

Give to us Eyes (using our eyes to really see)
No. 18 in *Someone's Singing Lord* (2nd Edition), published by A&C Black, 2002.

Quiet reflection or prayer

For a universal, humanistic or multi-faith assembly:

Quiet reflection

The assembly leader says:

'Close your eyes and picture Jack and Jimbo practising their dives. (Pause) We have to practise to get good at something. Think of something you would like to be good at and decide to practise. (Pause) Think of something you like doing and are good at already, and decide to practise to get even better. (Pause) Think of what you can do to be fit and healthy. (Pause) Finally, think about what a good friend Jimbo was. Think about how you could be helpful to someone today.' (Pause)

Or for Christian schools:

Prayer

Heavenly Father,
Help us to work hard to improve our skills and thank you for giving us life and health. Help us, too, in making healthy choices about exercise and healthy eating. Finally, dear Father, help us to be good to our friends and kind to everyone.

Amen.

A Secret

Teacher's Notes

Theme Five (b)	Hidden Disability
Inclusive Education:	Developing empathy for children who may have a hidden disability is part of **Inclusive Education**

Children may have disabilities that are not immediately obvious. If a child has a hidden disability they should feel comfortable to tell others if they so choose. Children who are confided in need to learn to be empathetic, understanding and discreet.

Lesson Plan

This five-part lesson plan is only a guide. Teachers are likely to add to or amend the learning activities which are suggested and may sometimes wish to substitute their own. For any part of the session they may wish to allow more or less time than that suggested.

1 Introduce the theme *5 minutes*

Two girls' friendship is tested when a secret comes between them.

2 Vocabulary *5 minutes*

The teacher ensures that the children understand the words given – usually within the context of the story as it is being read.

3 The story *5–10 minutes*

The teacher shows the illustration and reads the story.

4 Talking about the story *10–15 minutes*

The teacher uses some of the questions and discussion points given, stimulating the children to talk about the story/theme.

5 The learning activity *20–25 minutes*

Learning activities are suggested. One could be selected and others used in subsequent, follow-up lessons.

Total time	*45–60 minutes*

1 INTRODUCE THE THEME

Key points

- You or children that you know may have a hidden disability. If children choose to tell someone else about their disability they should feel 'safe' in doing so and also know that the children told will show kindness and keep their secret.

2 VOCABULARY

Use your usual methods for introducing new words.

The difficult words/references in the story are:

reeled off	–	*recited, or made a verbal list*
anticipate	–	*to expect something and be ready for it*
betrayed	–	*to have harmed, or been unkind to someone rather than supported them*
cajoling	–	*coaxing or trying to persuade*
HIV virus	–	*a virus that infects human cells and uses the energy and nutrients in those cells to grow and multiply*
AIDS	–	*a condition where the body's immune system breaks down and is unable to fight off certain infections and illnesses*
fragile	–	*easy to break or damage*

3 THE STORY:

A Secret

A Secret

Alisha and Emily were the closest of friends. They sat together in class at school and played together at break times and almost always spent part of each weekend with each other, practising their dancing or playing with each other's hair. Alisha was tall, with dark skin and brown eyes that sparkled with life, she kept her hair in tiny plaits with rainbow coloured beads at the end. Emily had long blonde hair, brown eyes and a smile to make the sternest of people melt. When the girls saw each other, it was a bit like seeing a part of themselves – a sense of familiarity – a comfortable feeling.

It made no sense then, when Emily didn't want to join Alisha on holiday for a week during the summer. Alisha had been so excited about asking Emily. It had been her mum, Esther's suggestion. They were both going to London to visit relatives there and mum thought that Emily would enjoy the trip too.

Alisha had almost knocked some of the infant children over as she had raced into school with the news. She had stood in front of Emily gasping for breath, blurting out the invitation with such joy, such enthusiasm. And it all fell flat; completely flat. Like a balloon bright and full of air, and then; no more. There was a flicker of sadness on Emily's face as she made up an excuse. And Alisha *knew* it was an excuse because they had talked about what they would do in the summer holidays and Emily had very few plans.

"I thought you'd be as excited as me Emily, what's the matter with you?"

"I'm sorry Alisha, I *do* want to play with you, but I *don't* want to go away."

"Do you think your mum and dad will say no, or something? You're saying no to me without even asking?"

"I *am* saying no Alisha, please don't ask me any more questions!"

Emily ran off into the classroom and there was no more opportunity to talk.

At playtime, Alisha avoided Emily, she felt too upset. She decided to latch onto some other children who were skipping.

Emily sat on the bench, looking into the distance. She looked like she was somewhere else. The teacher checked she was OK and tried to encourage her to join in the skipping, but was quickly distracted by an argument that had broken out between two younger children.

The day continued with lots of awkwardness between Alisha and Emily and it didn't help that everyone seemed to notice. Well, it *was* unusual when the two girls weren't in each other's pockets.

After school, Alisha managed to hold herself together until she got home and then she threw herself onto her mum in floods of tears.

"What's gone wrong with you today little missie?" mum asked.

She tried to prise Alisha away from her to see her face, but Alisha kept clinging on.

"Did you get into trouble or something? Tell me Alisha."

Alisha shook her head as mum reeled off a possible list of what she thought *might* have gone wrong during the day.

Eventually the storm of tears quietened itself and Alisha found the words.

"Emily d... d... don't want to come to London with us."

Alisha started to cry again and her mum tried to calm her, by offering her a drink.

They sat together on the sofa; Esther's brain was racing trying to anticipate why Emily had not wanted to come.

"Maybe Emily doesn't like big cities Alisha, not everyone likes how busy it is. Or ... or perhaps she knows that her mum and dad want her to be around for some reason."

Whatever mum suggested, Alisha wasn't convinced. Alisha felt betrayed, confused and very hurt.

"OK, how 'bout if I phone Emily's mum. Maybe she'll be able to explain."

Alisha nodded.

"You can watch that new video, if you like." Again Alisha nodded.

Alisha's mum took the phone upstairs and it seemed to Alisha that she had disappeared for ages.

Eventually mum popped her head round the door.

"C'mon Alisha, we're off to Emily's house."

Alisha, not surprisingly, wasn't very pleased, but with some cajoling, she was persuaded to put her jacket on.

They walked without talking, Alisha wondering what she would say to Emily. By the time they arrived at the house Alisha felt nervous, although she couldn't explain why.

Anna opened the door and flashed a warm smile at both Alisha and her mum.

"Come in, come in. Good to see you Esther, and you Alisha. Come and sit down and I'll get us all a drink."

Emily was nowhere to be seen. Alisha was even more nervous, but perhaps a little bit relieved too.

"Now, I think I have some explaining to do to you Alisha." Another warm smile and suddenly Alisha felt less nervous and more curious.

"Emily thinks you are the *best* friend she has *ever* had, you know. And you two seem as close as sisters when I see you together. But Emily hasn't told you everything about herself you know, because sometimes secrets are hard to share – even with your best friends. Alisha … Emily has the HIV virus … have you heard of it?"

Alisha nodded a yes.

"Well, it means that she has to take a *lot* of tablets to keep her healthy. She was frightened that if she came to London with you, you'd find out, and stop being friends with her. Lots of children and grown ups can get treated differently when they tell someone that they have HIV you see. Alisha picked up the virus from me and I don't always get treated kindly."

"But she knows that it wouldn't matter to me – I'm her best friend!"

"I'm glad it doesn't matter to you Alisha, but in Emily's last school some children found out who she *thought* were her friends and they started to ignore her. They even wrote messages telling her not to touch anybody in case she gave them AIDS. Kids can be very cruel or very kind, just like adults really, and you can't always work out which way people will fall over certain things."

Alisha had masses of questions to ask, but most of all she wanted to see Emily.

"Can I see Emily please, Anna?"

Anna led Alisha upstairs. There were some sobbing noises coming from the bedroom.

Anna slowly opened the door. "Alisha wants to see you Emily."

"You go in, she'll be OK." Anna nodded reassuringly to Alisha and disappeared downstairs.

"Emily, it's OK y'know, your mum told me about you having HIV. I don't know much about it, but I know it's not easy to catch and I *know* that I still want to be friends with you. It can be our secret. You don't have to tell anyone who doesn't need to know."

Emily stopped crying, and looked up. She looked so sad, so fragile. She couldn't manage a smile, but she sat up on the bed and looked Alisha in the eyes, as if she were looking for something.

"Are you sure you're still my friend …?"

"I'm as sure 'bout that as I am that I hate carrots!"

Both girls laughed.

"I'm sure too that you can't catch HIV from a hug."

Alisha threw her arms round her fragile friend and gave her an enormous hug.

"So are you coming to London, or what?"

"If mum says it's OK I'd love to!"

The girls, with arms linked, walked downstairs.

The mums were still chatting and Esther was holding some leaflets that Anna had given her about HIV.

"Emily, will you come to London with us? We'll do our homework, so that we look after you properly! Look at all these leaflets your mum has given me! My bedtime reading!"

"Yes please, I'd love to go!" Emily beamed at Esther.

Alisha and Emily gave each other another huge hug to celebrate.

4 TALKING ABOUT THE STORY

Did the children understand?

- Why was Alisha so excited at the beginning of the story?

- Why did she quickly become so upset and confused?

- What is HIV? (It stands for 'human immunodeficiency virus', and infects human cells.)

- Why did Emily not feel able to tell Alisha about having HIV at first?

Points for discussion

- Secrets should be kept out of *choice* – rather than out of *fear* of how someone will respond.

- If a child or friend shared a personal secret with you – what would be the best way to respond?

5 THE LEARNING ACTIVITY

Links

i)   The activities link with the story through the focus on keeping secrets and learning about HIV.

ii) The assembly connects with the story through a consideration of children's responses to someone with a hidden disability.

iii) If you wish to link the activity to the assembly, one or more of the children could read aloud their chosen poem. Some of the children's role-plays could be performed.

ACTIVITY SUGGESTIONS

I CHOOSING AN ACTIVITY LINKED TO THE STORY

(A) Let the children:

- Draw a picture to illustrate a part of the story that sticks in your mind.

or

- Write a conversation between two friends, where one is telling the other a secret. (You could set it out like a play with the names at the side of your paper.)

(B) Poetry:

- Write a poem about a child who wants to share a secret, but is afraid to.

or

- In pairs or in small groups, find a poem or song which connects with the story. It could be about disability, friendship or secrets.

Resources needed

Poetry and/or song books

2 INFORMATION ABOUT HIV/AIDS

Some, or all, of the following information can be shared and discussed with the children, depending on their age. It is important that the teacher focuses on two things:

1   HIV is not easy to pass on to others;
2   a child is not to blame for having HIV, and should be treated with the same kindness and respect as all other children.

- HIV stands for the Human Immune Deficiency Virus.

- The virus prevents the body's immune system from working properly. It infects 'helper' cells in the body and uses them to grow and reproduce (multiply).

- AIDS stands for Acquired Immune Deficiency Syndrome. It is not a disease in itself, but a condition where the body can be infected with a number of infections like pneumonia or tuberculosis, which take advantage of the body's weakened immune system.

- HIV is not easy to pass from one person to another. It can only be transmitted through certain body fluids like blood or breast milk (this is how babies can be infected by their mothers).

- HIV cannot be passed through food or air (i.e. by sneezing or coughing). Neither can it be passed by hugging, sharing toilet or washing facilities, nor by using eating utensils or eating food handled by someone with HIV.

- For current additional information there are a number of websites; the following were used to collate the information above.

  www.savethechildren.org.uk
  www.nat.org.uk
  www.ukcoalition.org
  www.thebody.com/amfar

- In pairs, children could role-play a situation where one child is telling the other a personal secret (they have diabetes, they have to go to the hospital for tests, etc.).

Assembly

Theme: Hidden Disability and Keeping Secrets

Introduction

The assembly leader introduces the theme. We may be aware of disabilities that we can see, but sometimes disabilities or illnesses are less obvious. We need to learn how to respond with kindness and empathy to someone with a hidden disability.

Story

Assembly leader:

'Our story today is about a girl who doesn't feel able to tell her best friend a secret about herself.'

The assembly leader reads the story – *A Secret*.

Poem or song

You can choose a poem or a song or both. Alternatively, you can have a child (or children) read the poems they chose or wrote in class and have one of the songs that were chosen. Select poems and songs which are relevant to the theme or which echo the story in some way.

Examples

Poems:

That's you and me! (celebrating close friendship)
Page 7 in *Poems about You and Me: A collection of poems about values*, compiled by Brian Moses, published by Wayland Publishers, 1998.

Secrets (different sorts of secrets)
Page 16 in *Poems about You and Me: A collection of poems about values*, compiled by Brian Moses, published by Wayland Publishers, 1998.

I had no friends at all (finding a friend)
Page 18 in *A Very First Poetry Book*, compiled by John Foster, published by Oxford University Press, 1984.

Songs:

With a little help from my friends (the value of good friends)
No. 38 in *Alleluya!* (2nd Edition), published by A&C Black, 1980.

On life's highway (helping each other on life's journey)
No. 28 in *Every Colour Under the Sun*, published by Ward Lock Educational Co. Ltd, 1983.

Take care of a friend (showing kindness to friends and others)
No. 35 in *Every Colour Under the Sun*, published by Ward Lock Educational Co. Ltd, 1983.

Quiet reflection or prayer

For a universal, humanistic or multi-faith assembly:

Quiet reflection

The assembly leader says:
'One of your friends or classmates may have a secret. (Pause) They may have a hidden disability. If they chose to tell you about it, would you respond kindly? Imagine what you might say that would be caring and thoughtful. (Pause) Could you be trusted to keep a secret? (Pause) Be determined that you will be a trustworthy friend.' (Pause)

Or for Christian schools:

Prayer

Creator God,
Your love is in each of us. We thank you for that love. Help us to be aware that we may have friends or classmates with a hidden disability. Help us to share Your love with everyone by showing kindness and compassion. Help us to be helpful to our classmates and friends.

Amen.

Solo?

Teacher's Notes

Theme Six (a)   Families come in all kinds

Inclusive Education: Recognising that there are many
different kinds of families is part
of **Inclusive Education**

> **Our classroom activities should reflect the reality of modern society
> with its many different kinds of family structures. We should not
> assume that 'family' only refers to the traditional two parents with
> their natural children. There are one parent, foster, adoptive,
> extended and other kinds of family.**

Lesson Plan

This five-part lesson plan is only a guide. Teachers are likely to add to or amend the learning
activities which are suggested and may sometimes wish to substitute their own. For any part
of the session they may wish to allow more or less time than that suggested.

1 Introduce the theme   *5 minutes*

The story is about a single parent family and illustrates that the
most important thing in a family is love.

2 Vocabulary   *5 minutes*

The teacher ensures that the children understand the words given.

3 The story   *5–10 minutes*

The teacher shows the illustration and reads the story.

4 Talking about the story   *10–15 minutes*

The teacher uses some of the questions and discussion points given,
stimulating the children to talk about the story/theme.

5 The learning activity   *20–25 minutes*

Learning activities are suggested. One could be selected and others
used in subsequent, follow-up lessons.

| Total time | *45–60 minutes* |

1 INTRODUCE THE THEME

Key points

● Explain what we mean by a 'nuclear' or 'traditional' family. Explain that there are many other kinds of families. Give examples and ask the children for some too (e.g. one parent – mum; one parent – dad; families with step-mother or step-father; extended families; two mothers or two fathers; foster families, etc.).

2 VOCABULARY

Use your usual methods for introducing new words.

The difficult words/references in the story are:

scanned	–	*looked over an area; searched with your eyes; looked quickly through something for what you wanted*
expectantly	–	*hopefully; thinking that something will happen*
baton	–	*a conductor's stick*
spontaneous	–	*unplanned*
intensely	–	*deeply; strongly*
chaotic	–	*disorderly*
urgently	–	*straight away; needing to be done immediately*
daze	–	*trance; unable to think clearly; stunned*
blurted	–	*sudden speech*
concussion	–	*loss of consciousness; being unconscious for a short time from a hard knock on the head*

3 THE STORY:

Solo?

Solo?

I was in my usual position, second from the left in the back row. We were a bit squashed. Over the heads of the smaller girls I scanned the faces of the audience. They were raised expectantly and nearly every seat was taken.

'I'll sit on the left,' dad had said.

I searched along the rows on that side, front to back. Mostly it was mothers out there. Dad should be easy to spot – tall as he was and his face dark amidst all those pale ones. He wasn't there though. Perhaps he had meant on *his* left? I scanned the rows to my right. He wasn't there either.

There was a buzz of expectancy. It was almost time. I felt really anxious, and watched the far door, desperately hoping he would suddenly appear, would come just in time. But no. Miss Ford raised her baton, the audience stilled, and we began.

Our voices rose in the first carol of the afternoon Christmas concert.

'Silent Night. Holy Night.'

As I sang the peaceful words, I was angry inside. Dad had said he would come. For once he would take the afternoon off from the hospital where he worked. For once I didn't want to be the only kid with no parent turning up. I was singing a solo and I wanted him to be there. Right up until the moment of my solo I was hoping he would arrive, rushing in late. But he didn't. As Miss Ford raised her baton for me, I put my feelings to one side and sang my very best. At the end there was a moment of silence, and then the audience burst into spontaneous applause. I felt intensely disappointed. I had done well but he had missed it. I had to blink back my tears.

There's only me and my dad. Mum died when I was only a baby. I don't really remember her but dad has given me some photographs. She was a pretty, smiling lady. In some photographs she's wearing English dresses and in others she has Nigerian clothes. She looks friendly. I wish I could have sung for her. I was sure she would have been there for me. Not like dad.

People are always telling me how important he is. Doing serious operations on people and all that. But what about me? I bet I was the only one in the choir with no one there just for me. And he had promised! For my solo.

I kept on thinking all these things as we sang the rest of the carols. All the time I was thinking about dad. Actually, it wasn't like him not to keep a promise. Perhaps there had been an emergency or something. I knew, deep down, that he would have been there if he could. Suddenly I felt scared. What if he had been in an accident?

At the end of the concert, the other choir girls rushed down into the hall to greet their mothers. From the stage I watched this chaotic dance of people pushing and waving and calling. I felt outside it all, as though I was not really there – or there but invisible. I jumped when Miss Ford touched my arm.

'Isa, come with me dear. I have something to tell you.'

My heart squeezed with fear as I followed her.

'Is it my dad?' I said, urgently.

She didn't answer until we were in her office.

'He's had an accident,' she said. 'He's been taken to the hospital.'

Even though I had half guessed, my hand flew to my mouth and I gasped with shock.

Miss Ford patted my shoulder.

'We've no reason to think it's serious,' she said. 'Your aunt will know, she'll be here soon.'

I waited for my aunt in a daze. I felt sick. Someone brought me a cup of tea which I forgot to drink. I had never felt so afraid.

Apparently I waited only about ten minutes, but it seemed a very long time before my Aunt Lillian arrived. I was so pleased to see her. She gave me a hug.

'He's OK Isa,' she said, and relief, like waves of gentle music flowed through my veins. I couldn't say anything, but I hugged her back.

'He's had a few stitches and will be fine,' she said to Miss Ford. 'Some fool riding a bike on the pavement just outside …'

'Can I see him?' I blurted out.

'Of course, love,' said Aunt Lillian. 'We're going right now.'

'Give Dr Leyton my best wishes,' said Miss Ford, and Aunt Lillian drove me to the hospital. She's dad's sister, and very kind.

At the hospital we went to the accident section. The nurse on duty recognised me.

'Your dad's in Ward C, sweetheart,' she said. 'Don't look so worried. He's fine. Do him good to find out what it's like to be a patient,' she added, smiling.

Me and Aunt Lillian hurried to Ward C. We found dad in a little room off the ward, sitting in a chair, in a dressing gown, reading. There was a row of stitches like a pathway across his forehead.

Dad held out his arms as we entered and I ran into them. He gave me a long hug.

'Hello Lil,' he said, over my head. 'Thanks for coming.'

Aunt Lillian gave Dad various things she had brought for him.

'I'll have to go soon, Robert, for the kids,' she said. 'But Isa can stay. Len will come for her later.' She turned to me. 'You can stay with us tonight,' she said, 'and your dad will be home tomorrow.'

'Yes, I'm fine now actually, but we always keep people in overnight after a big bump on the head. Just in case of concussion. But my head's so hard it cracked the pavement,' he said, and we all laughed.

'But you are OK dad, aren't you?' I said, still a little bit worried.

'Don't worry my dear, I'm fine. I promise. I'm sorry I missed your concert though. The boy crashed into me just as I reached the school gate. Perishing pest. How did it go?'

'It went well, dad. Everyone clapped really hard. Which you're not supposed to do in a carol service.'

Dad laughed his deep laugh. 'I'll bet they did. He shook his head, slowly, from side to side. Wow, am I sorry I missed that!'

'It doesn't matter, dad,' I said. And suddenly I realised it was true. Nothing mattered, really, nothing at all. Just as long as dad was OK.

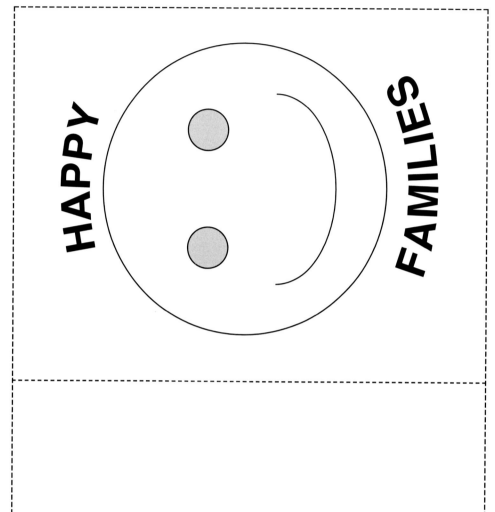

HAPPY

FAMILIES

To . . . .

Love from

Assembly

Theme: Families

Introduction

The assembly leader introduces the theme of families. There are many different kinds of families. A good family is one with lots of care given to everyone.

Story

Assembly leader:

'Our story today is about an accident in a caring one parent family in which the parent is a Dad.'

The assembly leader reads the story – *Solo?*

Poem or song

You can choose a poem or a song or both. Alternatively, you can have a child (or children) read the poems they chose or wrote in class and have one of the songs that were chosen. Select poems and songs which are relevant to the theme or which echo the story in some way.

Examples

Poems:

Me (the superstar in the family!)
Page 8 in *A Second Poetry Book*, compiled by John Foster, published by Oxford University Press, 1980.

Orders of the Day (gran – a special family member)
Page 16 in *A Second Poetry Book*, compiled by John Foster, published by Oxford University Press, 1980.

Never a Dull Moment (a lively, noisy family)
Page 12 in *Smile Please!* by Tony Bradman, published by Puffin, 1989.

Songs:

We Will Take Care of You (caring for a little baby)
No. 33 in *Every Colour Under the Sun*, published by Ward Lock Educational Co. Ltd, 1983.

There's Room Enough for You (your friend is also your family)
No. 33 in *Every Colour Under the Sun*, published by Ward Lock Educational Co. Ltd, 1983.

Father We Thank You for the Night (about loving care)
No. 1 in *Someone's Singing Lord* (2nd Edition), published by A&C Black, 2002.

I'm Very Glad of God (God a father)
No. 22 in *Someone's Singing Lord* (2nd Edition), published by A&C Black, 2002.

Quiet reflection or prayer

For a universal, humanistic or multi-faith assembly:

Quiet reflection

The assembly leader says:
'Close your eyes and think with gratitude of all those who give care to you. (Pause) Resolve that you will try to be a caring person too. (Pause) Think of someone to whom you can show kindness and care today.' (Pause)

Or for Christian schools:

Prayer

Dear Father,
We thank you for being our loving Father and for our earthly family too. Help us to be a kind and caring member of our family and to appreciate that all people, everywhere, are part of Your family too.

Amen.

Trainers
Teacher's Notes

Theme Six (b)	Parental Difference (a low-income family)
Inclusive Education:	Developing respect for differences in families is part of **Inclusive Education**

> **Parents from low-income families may not have the same opportunities to buy brand new clothes for their children, but a loving family is not dependent on the level of income.**

Lesson Plan

This five-part lesson plan is only a guide. Teachers are likely to add to or amend the learning activities which are suggested and may sometimes wish to substitute their own. For any part of the session they may wish to allow more or less time than that suggested.

1 Introduce the theme *5 minutes*

A boy is unfairly judged by one of his classmates because of the second-hand clothes that he wears. The story demonstrates that strength of character and determination is much more important than the clothes we wear.

2 Vocabulary *5 minutes*

The teacher ensures that the children understand the words given – usually within the context of the story as it is being read.

3 The story *5–10 minutes*

The teacher shows the illustration and reads the story.

4 Talking about the story *10–15 minutes*

The teacher uses some of the questions and discussion points given, stimulating the children to talk about the story/theme.

5 The learning activity *20–25 minutes*

Learning activities are suggested. One could be selected and others used in subsequent, follow-up lessons.

Total time *45–60 minutes*

1 INTRODUCE THE THEME

Key points

● Families have all kinds of differences and those differences are to be respected. Differences in family income may not always be evident, but where there is a low income, children are not likely to enjoy the material benefits that their peers might appreciate. It is important that a lack of material belongings, clothing or otherwise, is not used as a negative judgement of appearance or of the parent's care.

2 VOCABULARY

Use your usual methods for introducing new words.

The difficult words/references in the story are:

Noah	–	*a reference to the Old Testament character who built a large boat in response to God's command*
ark	–	*the large boat that Noah built for protection in the story of the ancient flood*
tentative	–	*rather hesitant*
'chomping at the bit'	–	*an expression that means that someone is eager to start something (a horse chomps at the bit in its mouth when eager to start racing)*
frantically	–	*doing something in a mad, furious or fast way*
Hermes	–	*a reference to the Greek messenger god who had wings on his feet*

THE STORY:

Trainers

Trainers

I didn't like Nicky from day one. He turned up in my class on the first day back after the Easter holidays. I knew he wouldn't fit in with my friends: he just didn't look right – do you know what I mean? His T-shirts were either too baggy or too tight, his tracksuit bottoms were full of holes and his trainers … well, Noah probably had a pair on the ark, they were that ancient! I didn't have anything against Nicky, but I decided from first glance that it would be a waste of time getting to know him.

Mrs Grey made the usual introductions, 'This is Nicky everyone, he's just moved into the area, please make him feel welcome.'

There happened to be a space next to me, because Raj was away – as bad luck would have it – so Nicky plonked himself down. He threw me a tentative smile with a quick 'Hi'. I nodded and managed a hello under my breath.

The morning passed quickly, as it sometimes does and lunchtime found me with my friend Ryan catching our breath after a manic game of football.

'You know there's going to be a race on Sports Day this year don't you Matt?' asked Ryan.

'Yeah! You enterin' then Ryan?' I questioned.

'Nah, more of a team player myself, I'll stick with the potted sports – plus I'm useless at running fast!'

'Doubt Nicky New Boy will be racing. Have you seen those trainers? They are off the ark, they are. He can hardly walk in them they're so big. He looks like an elephant with blisters on his feet, the way he walks!' Ryan and I exploded with laughter, glancing over at Nicky who was playing basketball on another part of the playground with a few of the other weird cases.

Nicky caught my eye, as if he guessed we were laughing at him. He gave me a strange look that embarrassed me, don't know why, maybe because it wasn't the 'daggers' look I expected.

I got through the rest of the day without having to sit next to Nicky which suited me fine. We had Technology which meant we were working in different groups. I have to admit that Nicky's group built a 'cool' bridge, probably down to Annette and Rohan (the two big brains of the class) being in the group, I thought.

I got to know about Nicky from other people in my class. I was curious about him even though I didn't want to talk to him myself. Nicky had moved into one of the flats opposite the video shop. His dad had to give up work to look after him and his brother and sister when his mum left.
'Money must be tight,' I thought smugly. 'No wonder his clothes look so weird.'

I know I'm lucky, I can persuade my mum to buy me most things if I catch her in the right mood. We don't have to worry about money and I like having the latest trainers and football shirt, it matters to me.

Although I'm only really into football, I was excited about Sports Day this year because of the optional races: a 50m or 80m sprint depending on your age. The potted sports were first – all team stuff. Then the sprints for those of us who wanted to run 'til our lungs were fit to burst.

I double-checked my kit before I left the house. I had my new trainers and the most 'wicked' football shirt I've ever had. Sports Day would be good.

'Got your kit for this afternoon then, Nicky?' I asked as we entered the classroom for register.

'Yeah, I'm wearing it, it saves time!' Nicky managed a smile, although I *know* I made him squirm a bit.

How did Nicky manage to keep his cool and look so uncool at the same time? I couldn't make sense of him and didn't really want to.

Potted Sports was the usual crazy but happy chaos with 150 children in teams of ten moving around fifteen different activities. Any grown ups who wanted to watch could follow a team round – some did and some spent all their time chatting, not having much of a clue what was going on. My mum gave me a wave from time to time. I threw her a half smile in return.

'Would children from Year 3 and 4 taking part in the 50m sprint make their way to Mr Evans at the start line please,' announced Mrs Croft, the head teacher, through the megaphone. Mr Evans was waving enthusiastically so that the children could find him

OK. I liked Mr Evans, he was always full of energy – like he had Lucozade on his cereal every morning or something. He had crazy clothes and a strange haircut, but when you've been in his class you get used to it.

Year 3 and 4 children lined up nervously on the start line. I was watching at the side with my class. We had a little 'pen' to sit in. I felt like a racehorse waiting to be released onto the track.

'On your marks … get set …' Bang! The gun went off and the children burst away from the start line. There were some good runners, I could see that. One of the girls ran as if she was being blown along, she made it look that easy! Her arms pumping the air just like the athletes you see on the TV.

Running, cheering then collapsing. The children sprawled over the finish line with Mrs Croft trying to sweep them away ready for the next race. My race and Nicky's race. I loved running so I was really up for the 80m sprint anyway, but with Nicky taking part I had a nagging doubt about the race. I felt I had something to prove. Why I felt threatened by Nicky I don't know, I didn't think he would get far in those trainers. Perhaps it was because he looked like a runner, he looked 'sporty' despite his kit not being fit for Oxfam.

'Year 5 and 6's 80m sprint will be the next race. Make your way over to Mr Evans as quickly as possible please,' blasted out Mrs Croft.

I jumped over the tape that had penned me in; I was raring to go, chomping at the bit. I glanced at Nicky who was having a word in Mr Evans' ear and getting huge, reassuring nods in return. Didn't know what that was about.

I lined up at the start taking a big breath. I looked across at the competition: Nina, Raj, Marcus, Annette, Rohan (they had brains and speed) and Nicky. Except Nicky wasn't on the start line yet. He was preoccupied with his trainers: he was taking them off – and his socks. Unbelievable! What was he playing at?

I looked back at the 'pen' and Ryan and I smirked at each other. We knew what we were thinking about the barefooted Nicky.

The Story

'Take your marks … get set …' Bang! We erupted from the start line almost in line with each other. I could feel the strength in my legs as I pounded the ground. Nina and Marcus started to pull away with me and Nicky. I know you're supposed to look ahead but I kept looking over frantically at Nicky. He was flying like that Greek god that has wings on his feet. I was pumping my arms, pounding my legs, panting for breath and I could not catch Nicky up. He had become someone else – that Greek god, Hermes is it? Born to run, or what. He was a blur of legs, arms and feet. Nicky threw himself through the tape at the finish line with Nina and Marcus and me closely behind (except not as closely as it should have been for a sprint!).

Couldn't help myself:

'Brilliant race Nicky – you really flew there! Are your feet OK?'

'Thanks, I really like running, but not in my trainers at the moment!'

Couldn't help myself again:

'Some of the Ethiopian athletes train in barefeet don't they? They're some of the best in the world.'

'Must be OK then,' laughed Nicky. 'And the Greek athletes used to run in the nude but I don't think I'll do that.' We both laughed.

I looked down at my trainers – they certainly were the coolest. I looked at Nicky as he jogged back to get his trainers. He had guts to run in barefeet. I could never have done that. Maybe I shouldn't give up on Nicky New Boy so quickly. I had a feeling that I would be the one to miss out!

4 TALKING ABOUT THE STORY

Did the children understand?

- Why does the narrator decide that Nicky is a 'waste of time' to get to know?

- How does Nicky embarrass the narrator on the playground?

- How does Nicky show his strength of character in the race?

Points for discussion

- A lack of money in a family does not necessarily equate with a lack of care.

- How can we check ourselves from judging by appearance (a natural thing to do in some ways)?

- Is it wrong to like new clothes?

- What might have happened to Nicky had he not had such a strong character?

5 THE LEARNING ACTIVITY

Links

i) The activities link with the story through the focus on respecting yourself and others irrespective of income.

ii) The assembly connects with the story through considering that good care is not related to income.

iii) If you wish to link the activity to the assembly, one or more of the children could read aloud their chosen poem. Drawings of Greek athletes could be shown or children could feedback key points from the circle time on 'caring'.

ACTIVITY SUGGESTIONS

I CHOOSING AN ACTIVITY LINKED TO THE STORY

(A) Let the children:

- Draw a picture of Nicky running in the race.

or

- Write a story from Nicky's perspective about his first day at his new school.

(B) Poetry:

● Write a poem about running and/or winning a race.

or

● Find a poem either individually or in a group which connects with the story. It could be about running, sports day, or families and caring.

Resources needed

Poetry and/or song books

2 THE ANCIENT GREEKS

Both Nicky and the narrator make reference to the Ancient Greeks. The narrator likens Nicky to Hermes – the messenger god – and Nicky jokes about not running without clothes like the Ancient Greeks. In pairs, or in a group, find out about the Ancient Greeks and their love of athletics or find out about the Greek gods. Each group could feed back to the class.

Resources needed

Reference books about Ancient Greece

3 CARING

In circle time ask the children to think about all the ways that they are shown care or can care for others which are *not* dependent on spending lots of money.

Assembly

Theme: Families

Introduction

The assembly leader introduces the theme. There are many different kinds of families. Good care doesn't depend on having lots of material possessions.

Story

Assembly leader:

'Our story today is about a boy called Nicky whose family doesn't have much money, and another boy's response to Nicky.'

The assembly leader reads the story – *Trainers*

Poem or song

You can choose a poem or a song or both. Alternatively, you can have a child (or children) read the poems they chose or wrote in class and have one of the songs that were chosen. Select poems and songs which are relevant to the theme or which echo the story in some way.

Examples

Poems:

The New Lad (a child starts school who is 'different')
Page 12 in *Poems about You and Me: A collection of poems about values*, compiled by Brian Moses, published by Wayland Publishers, 1998.

Going Barefoot (enjoying being without shoes – as Nicky does in the race)
Page 48 in *A First Poetry Book*, compiled by John Foster, published by Oxford University Press, 1979.

Never a Dull Moment (an example of family life)
Page 12 in *Smile Please!* by Tony Bradman, published by Puffin, 1989.

Songs:

Seeds of Kindness (kind behaviour makes us happy)
No. 42 in *Every Colour Under the Sun*, published by Ward Lock Educational Co. Ltd, 1983.

Such Hard Work (there is an effort involved in showing care to others)
No. 29 in *Every Colour Under the Sun*, published by Ward Lock Educational Co. Ltd, 1983.

Quiet reflection or prayer

For a universal, humanistic or multi-faith assembly:

Quiet reflection

The assembly leader says:
'Close your eyes for a moment and think about those people who care for you. (Pause) Think about what you most value from someone who cares for you – especially the care given that *isn't* dependent on buying you 'things'. (Pause) Think about ways in which you can show appreciation for the care given to you.' (Pause)

Or for Christian schools:

Prayer

Dear God,
Thank you that Your loving care surrounds us. Teach us to appreciate the care shown to us, from family and friends. Help us to know that true caring is dependent on love rather than money. Help us to respect each other however much or little money our families might have. Teach us to show Your loving care to others.

Amen.